"Bishop Erik Varden offers a lively and fresh view of today's world, of which he knows very well literature, art, and cinema. To this post-secular but not post-Christian age, he declares sympathy and trust because Christ, Alpha and Omega, is at the beginning and will be at the end of history."
—**Giovanni Maria Vian**, former editor-in-chief of *L'Osservatore Romano*

"What burns at the heart of each chapter in *Towards Dawn*, along with the light and fire of a fine, contemplative intelligence, is a flame of faith that, far from being cowed by the grim, unhappy winds of modern secularization, survives and thrives with a fire of conviction at once notably urgent and yet always serene. In a reflection on contemporary society from a spiritual perspective, it's hard to imagine a more illumined, more authoritative statement than these few lines from the preface: 'It is often casually said that we live in post-Christian times. I believe that statement to be false. Theologically, the term "post-Christian" makes no sense. Christ is the Alpha and the Omega, and all the letters in between. He carries constitutionally the freshness of morning dew. Christianity is of the dawn.'"
—**Father Paul Murray, OP**, author of *A Journey with Jonah* and *Light at the Torn Horizon*

"At the beginning of the third millennium, Pope Saint John Paul II prophetically stated that the bishop is called 'to be a prophet, witness, and servant of hope . . . instilling confidence and proclaiming before all people the basis of Christian hope' (*Pastores gregis* 3). Bishop Erik Varden fulfills this essential duty in this collection of essays. As a man of hope, he thoughtfully reflects on important concerns for the contemporary Church and society, avoiding idealistic optimism and nihilistic pessimism. He builds his reflections on the rock of Jesus Christ, the Truth, and offers the reader profound reasons for hope amid the contemporary cries for meaning and purpose. The book is timely as we celebrate one of the final gifts given to the Church and the world by Pope Francis: the Jubilee Year of Hope."
—**Archbishop Samuel J. Aquila**, archbishop of Denver

Praise for *Towards Dawn*

"Bishop Erik Varden is one of the great confessors of the faith in our time. In this collection of essays, he weaves together spiritual wisdom from the Scriptures, the tradition of the Church, the lives of the saints, and classical and contemporary literature. He notes that Christianity is premised on the irruption of eternity in time and thus that essential coordinates are and must remain constant. As the Carthusian motto declares, *Stat crux dum volvitur orbis*—The cross stands firm while the world turns. He concludes that 'we need a Christocentric conversion in mind and manners to make sense of our significant being, to account for our origin and end, our longings and frustrations, our wounds and our capacity for healing.' This is a very hopeful book."

—**Tracey Rowland**, St. John Paul II Chair of Theology, University of Notre Dame (Australia), member of the Pontifical Academy of Social Sciences

"Bishop Erik Varden is the most exquisite and enthralling Catholic writer of our day, leery of the twin temptations of craven modernity and frozen traditionalism, always digging deep into the past and finding renewal and refreshment to meet the needs of the present."

—**Brendan Walsh**, editor of *The Tablet*

"In these dark times, we are profoundly in need of hope. Bishop Erik Varden's searching reflections deliver. With wit and wisdom, he rightly diagnoses the modern world's problem—our alienation from our own bodies (see chapter 3)—and provides the only true solution: 'The embodied application of Christian faith in God's Incarnation.' You will come away understanding all the more what Vatican II meant in declaring that 'only in the mystery of the Incarnate Word does the mystery of man take on light.'"

—**Christopher West**, president of the Theology of the Body Institute

TOWARDS DAWN

TOWARDS DAWN

ESSAYS IN HOPEFULNESS

BISHOP ERIK VARDEN

W✦RD on FIRE

Published by Word on Fire, Elk Grove Village, IL 60007
© 2025 by Erik Varden
Printed in Italy
All rights reserved

Cover design, typesetting, and interior art direction by Nic Fredrickson, Clark Kenyon, and Rozann Lee

Scripture excerpts are from the New Revised Standard Version Bible: Catholic Edition (copyright © 1989, 1993), used by permission of the National Council of the Churches of Christ in the United States of America.
All rights reserved worldwide.

Excerpt from the English translation of the *Catechism of the Catholic Church* for use in the United States of America copyright © 1994, United States Catholic Conference, Inc.—Libreria Editrice Vaticana. Used by permission. English translation of the *Catechism of the Catholic Church*: Modifications from the Editio Typica copyright © 1997, United States Conference of Catholic Bishops—Libreria Editrice Vaticana.

No part of this book may be used or reproduced in any manner whatsoever without written permission, except in the case of brief quotations in critical articles or reviews. For more information, contact Word on Fire Catholic Ministries, PO Box 97330, Washington, DC 20090-7330 or email contact@wordonfire.org.

ISBN: 978-1-68578-274-0

Library of Congress Control Number: 2025935901

Contents

Preface	ix
1. Evangelisation in Forgetful Times	1
2. Can Literature Save Lives?	23
3. The Body at Prayer	40
4. The Monastery as *SCHOLA DEI*	57
5. Repairing the Wound	75
6. 'Be Holy!': The Scandal of Sanctity	85
7. Synodality and Holiness	105
8. Setting 'Spirituality' Free	116
9. On Blessings	121
10. Confirmation	127
Notes	133

Preface

It is often casually said that we live in post-Christian times. I believe that statement to be false. Theologically, the term 'post-Christian' makes no sense. Christ is the Alpha and the Omega, and all the letters in between. He carries constitutionally the freshness of morning dew. Christianity is of the dawn.

If at times, during given periods, we feel enshrouded by twilight, it is because another day is in the making. It seems to me clear that we find ourselves in such a process of awakening now. If we do want to deal in the currency of 'pre' and 'post', I think it more apposite to suggest that we stand on the threshold of an age I would call 'post-secular'.

Secularisation has run its course. It is exhausted, void of positive finality. The human being, meanwhile, remains alive with deep aspirations. It is an essential task of the Church to listen to these attentively, with respect, then to orient them towards Christ, who carries the comfort and challenge for which the human heart yearns.

The essays in this volume attempt to read the signs of our times hopefully. Hope, it should be noted, is not the same as optimism.

Christianity is no utopianism. Biblical religion is supremely, in some ways shockingly, realistic. The great teachers of faith have always insisted that supernatural life must build on a true appraisal of nature. We must train ourselves to see things as they are, ourselves as we are: spiritual life presupposes ability and courage to call a spade a spade.

To have Christian hope is not to expect everything to work out all right. Not everything does. To hope is to have confidence that everything, even suffering, disappointment, and injustice, can be purposeful. The light 'shines in the darkness' (John 1.5). It does not obliterate the dark – yet; that will be for the new heaven and the new earth, in which 'there will be no more night' (Revelation 22.5). Here and now, hope glimmers.

That is not to say it is inconsequential. There is a blessed contagion in hope, enabling it to spread from heart to heart. Totalitarian powers always work to obliterate hope and induce despair. That is significant. To school ourselves in hope is to exercise ourselves in freedom. In a wonderful poem, Péguy describes hope as the flame of the sanctuary lamp. This flame, he says, 'has traversed the depths of all the night'. It lets us see what is now, yet envisage what may come about. To hope is to stake one's existence on the possibility of becoming. That is an art to practise with assiduity today, in the fatalist, determinist atmosphere of our so very strange times.

This year the Catholic Church celebrates a jubilee under the motto *Peregrinantes in spem*. The phrase is dynamic. The word 'hope', *spes*, is in the accusative, designating it as the reality towards which we move as towards our natural home, much as the prodigal son of the parable, shocked to find himself enclosed in all-encompassing estrangement, 'came to himself' (Luke 15.17), then set out without delay towards his father's house. To be pilgrims in progress towards hope is to move out of meaninglessness perceived towards sense and purpose incarnate in Christ, God from God, Light from Light.

Day is breaking. Why turn away from it disorientedly?

+fr Erik Varden
Ascension 2025

I

Evangelisation in Forgetful Times

Among the earliest outpourings of the human spirit to have been passed down to us is the *Epic of Gilgamesh*. Gilgamesh was king of Uruk, on the bank of the Euphrates, around 2800 BC, when the Sumerian city-states knew their first flourishing. The oldest collections of Gilgamesh poems, preserved on clay tablets, date from around 2000 BC. Their various strands were woven together in different languages and places over eight hundred years to reach their standard epic form around 1200 BC.

Issued from a goddess's embraces with a man, Gilgamesh was a mortal, though sufficiently imbued with divinity to yearn for everlasting life. This yearning – undirected, thus frustrated – expressed itself in fierce enterprise and boundless ambition. Gilgamesh exhausted the people of Uruk, who pleaded with the gods to fashion a hero who might absorb their king's unrest: 'Let him be a match for the storm of his heart', they prayed, 'let them vie with each other, so Uruk may be rested!' The answer to this prayer was Enkidu, a man of preternatural ability, who won Gilgamesh's friendship. Together they travelled to the ends of the earth, set on adventure, each a source of courage and comfort to the other.

Enkidu's death provoked a crisis in Gilgamesh. His reluctance to surrender the body of his friend to the tomb made the transience of human existence disturbingly apparent: 'I did not surrender his body for burial', says Gilgamesh, 'until a maggot dropped from his nostril.' This, he realised, was the fate in store for him also. He could not bear to sit and wait for it. So he began to roam, fleeing reminders of mortality:

> I was afraid that I too would die, . . .
> what became of my friend Enkidu was too
> much to bear,
> so on a far path I wander the wild.

Gilgamesh raced against the sun. He sought out Uta-napishti, Babylon's Noah, survivor of the Flood; he dived to the bottom of the sea to pick a youth-restoring plant, which a serpent then slithered away with. All the while the gods called out, 'Gilgamesh, where are you wandering? The life that you seek you never will find.' At the end of the epic, we find Gilgamesh back in Uruk, before the city wall he had built. Gilgamesh regarded that monumental wall as his one claim to immortality.

It has perished, of course, as surely as did the works of Shelley's Ozymandias. The word alone, apparently fugacious yet wondrously able to bridge the distance of four thousand years, allows Gilgamesh to live among us still – a near, strangely troubling presence.

I say 'troubling' because Gilgamesh could be our contemporary. He is a megalomaniac, in love with his proficiency but unsure of his purpose, haunted by death, perplexed by his heart's craving, courageous in the face of the absurd, yet weighed down by sadness. Especially striking is Gilgamesh's refusal to stay still. The keener his despair, the more frantic his movement: Remember, he attempted to outrun the course of the sun. This tendency is as old as humanity. Yet never have women and men been so well equipped to indulge it as today.

The modern fixation with movement and change is dissected in a 2018 book by François-Xavier Bellamy, a notable figure in French political and intellectual life – two arenas that do not, perhaps, intersect often enough. Bellamy maintains that a gradual transformation of consciousness began in the wake of the scientific revolution wrought by Copernicus and Galileo. Whereas Gilgamesh knew human contingency within a world supposed to be stable, we moderns regard change as a universal law. We take it for granted that nothing endures, that we are specks of dust in an expanding universe, that reality as such is advancing with no set goal, having no centre. The one thing left to believe in is movement or 'progress'. We pursue it religiously. The ideologies of the twentieth century made of progress an absolute value. The market economy is based upon it. It increasingly establishes its sway in anthropology. The narrative of 'transhumanism' no longer pertains to Orwellian hyperbole. It is put before us as the inevitable next stage of 'progress', which some predict will see human beings outdone by the machine. So completely have we succumbed to this manner of thinking, notes Bellamy, that 'modernity is characterised by an immense rage against anyone who declines to fall into step with its rhythm'. Our passion for change has become obsessive and totalitarian.

We encounter this passion in the Church too. It accounts for major tensions that plague the ecclesial body to the extent of threatening its unity. It is surely an ecclesial task to make the Word of God intelligible *now* while remaining faithful to an unbroken tradition. The Word of God does not speak into a void but to minds and hearts, eliciting a response. Its expositors must address real people, the people of their time. Yet how do we get our message across? By what approaches, images, and terms can the Church's *kerygma* be made resplendent in our fast-moving time, conveyed 'not as a human word but as what it really is, God's word' (1 Thessalonians 2.13), as a decisive *evangelion*? What is the freeing word our world longs to hear? What, in our contemporaries' anguish, is essential, what merely of the hour? To answer such questions is to identify an ecclesial and evangelical task. It exceeds my presumption to pretend to do so in the course of an essay. What I shall attempt is simpler.

First, I shall suggest four perspectives on evangelisation by reflecting on the semantic potential of the word 'catholic', a word qualifying our theological enterprise and announcing our mission. Next, I shall consider a curious feature of today's Catholic climate, at least in the Western world: the tendency by which the very elderly call the young retrograde and conflicts arise over the rightful custody of tradition. Intergenerational squabbles about what to keep in the attic and what to bring down are banal. They occur in every age. Here and now, though, they are peculiarly charged, conditioned by a verifiable experience of rupture. Considering this rupture serenely, we may hope – this is my third section – to bring to it, too, an *evangelion* in view of healing. This matter is of concern to me. Perhaps it may concern you also.

WHAT IS CATHOLIC?

The adjective 'catholic' reaches us through Latin from Greek, where we find it as an adverb, *kath' holon*, meaning 'according to the whole'. Aristotle opposes what is *kath' holon* to what is *kath' hekaston*, 'pertaining to specifics'. It is 'catholic' to contain a sum of particulars and to form them into an elegant whole. In this regard, I am indebted to Dame Gertrude Brown, a nun of Stanbrook, for a brilliant insight. In the early 1980s, she was sent to the United States to assist a community reconciled to the Church after embroilment in what came to be called the Boston heresy case. Dame Gertrude was glad to accompany a broadening of outlook among the sisters and brothers. One day she wrote home to Stanbrook delightedly. A homily preached that morning at Mass, she noted, had been 'very good. Marks of true Christian spirituality – Trinitarian, Christocentric, Biblical, doctrinal, liturgical, Catholic, *i.e.* hospitable.' I consider this definition of 'Catholic' as 'hospitable' to be inspired. To be a Catholic is to inhabit a vast, inviting space and to breathe within it an air of Alpine freshness. A construct of theology in which we keep bumping our head on the ceiling, oppressed by the odour of old socks, may need to be tested for catholicity. That said, to be hospitable is to invite guests *home*, and a home has boundaries. What is more, a home is a space that is lived in and loved. To claim a home as home, it is not enough just to be able to itemise its furniture; we must use it, cherish it, make it our own. A Catholic theologian is one who receives the Catholic tradition in its fullness with a guest's graciousness, increasingly grateful to find a home within it and delighting in inviting others in, to enable their homecoming also.

A second hallmark, outlined in the so-called 'canon' of Vincent of Lérins, is this: Catholic truth is what has been believed everywhere, always, and by all. This is not to contend that theology is static, but to say that theology's *object* does not change. This object is given, revealed, and calls for reverence. Theology aspiring to be Catholic may not be reoriented to lesser causes. We should beware of projects that set out to develop a theology 'of' this or that; likewise of attempts to tie theology down by descriptive, identity-political tags. Theology is the intelligent, humble, praying engagement with the deposit of faith handed down in the Church – nothing less. When the Church tries to keep up with passing fashions, she is bound to fail. She will always lag a few steps behind. She risks cutting a sorry, even comical figure, like late-middle-aged parents who attempt to adopt the dress code of their teenage children. This fact reveals the fragility of in-*sub*-culturation. It teaches us that Catholic engagement with contemporary culture must touch the still waters of the depths, not the flotsam washed up on beaches.

To consider a third aspect of the word 'catholic', let us return to Aristotle's definition. To be *kath' holon*, says he, is to generate a whole out of disparate parts. This presupposes an ability to hold a degree of tension. The key dogmas of our faith (of the Trinity, the hypostatic union, the body's resurrection) are vastly sophisticated formulas of equilibrated paradox. The encompassing nature of Catholic thought requires of those who exercise it a well-formed, rigorous discipline of mind. The Catholic theologian must be learned in the Scriptures, which he or she should ideally study in the languages of their composition; he or she must be conversant with philosophy both ancient and modern, have a good grasp of history, understand the form and development of doctrine, and be able to pursue Catholic truth, not only in manuals, but in the

Gradual and Missal, and in hagiography. At a time when faculties of theology are pushed out of universities, it is vital to uphold the intellectual integrity of the discipline. Sociologists tell us that the residual transmission of faith within communities is, in the West, a model in collapse. The believer of the future is likely to have made a solitary journey to faith by way of a searching mind. The intellectual apostolate plays a key part in displaying the coherence and beauty of Catholic teaching, in stimulating minds moulded by computational logic to metaphysical flights.

While Catholic theology challenges and satisfies the intellect, it is not restricted to discursive forms. It appeals to our whole being. It engages our sensibility. To illustrate this fourth characteristic of catholicity, I will call on a testimony from outside the fold, as it were. A few years ago, Navid Kermani, the German Orientalist and novelist, published a book of essays on Christian art. It is a book remarkable for its insight – even more for the fact that its author, of Iranian descent, is a Shia Muslim. With empathy and acumen, Kermani reflects on how the Catholic soul has sought pictorial expression over the centuries. He makes original, shrewd observations because he has that distance from the subject which enables a global view, alert to the strangeness of motifs that Christians, blinded by familiarity, fail to notice. In one essay, Kermani makes an especially significant statement. While prolonged engagement with Christian creativity did not convert him, he writes, it led him to 'recognise, or better still, to *feel*, why Christianity is a possibility.' In order to unlock that door of perception, double-bolted in an atheistic age, the Church's heritage of music, visual art, and the *ars celebrandi* may be at least as effective as a multitude of words, as was the case with Saint Augustine in Milan or, five centuries later, with Prince

Vladimir's envoys to the Constantinopolitan court. In this area, too, stringent standards must be met. Where the communication of truth is at stake, there is no room for mediocrity. Integrity of worship will overflow in charity to the poor and in peace-making on evangelical terms, grounded in justice.

Catholic theology, then, is compassionate and open-minded, yet has clearly thought-out boundaries; it constantly reroots itself in divine revelation and the deposit of faith in order, therefrom, to find adequate and supernatural responses to contemporary quandaries; 'compact in itself' (see Psalm 122.3), firm in its core, it has the solidity required to sustain intellectual tension and to enunciate a coherent, confident account of the hope with which it is entrusted; it endeavours to express this hope, which draws mankind out of self-referentiality towards participation in the divine nature (see 2 Peter 1.4), not only in discursive teaching, but in art, in the celebration of the mystery of faith, and in just charity.

THE AGGIORNAMENTO OF ANOTHER DAY

None of this is controversial in principle. Controversy comes sailing in from another angle. Much talk about what is and is not Catholic is presently conducted not on the basis of principles but on the basis of sensibility. Here disagreements are rife. Permit me to make my point anecdotally. Early in 2018, while abbot of a monastery in England, I asked for a life of Paul VI to be read in the refectory, to accompany the brethren's dinner. Paul VI was to be canonised that autumn. It seemed opportune to revisit his life and career. We had in our library the standard English account, *Paul VI: The First Modern Pope* by Peter Hebblethwaite, so that was the volume we chose.

After the first instalment had been read, one of our young monks, a man of good sense in his twenties, came to see me. He observed that the author, introducing his subject, had used the accolade 'modern' three times on the first half-page. I checked. He was right. Hebblethwaite calls Paul VI a 'modern pope' and 'modern man', and he adds that he was 'modern' above all by implementing Vatican II.

This language says more about the author than about his subject. Hebblethwaite was born in 1930. Having become a Jesuit in 1948, he spent a quarter-century in the Society before leaving it to marry. He remained into old age a prolific commentator on Church matters. He would very much have thought himself a 'modern' man. In his introduction to the life of Papa Montini, he exudes the confidence of a 'modern' Catholic. This confidence is bound up with the reception of the council. Hebblethwaite is sure he knows what is right in this respect; he is sure he understands what the council *really* means. He fulminates against the pope in office at the time of publication – that is, in the year of our Lord 1993. The man we now venerate as Pope Saint John Paul II was to Hebblethwaite a repudiator of Paul VI's policies, a dismantler of Montini's heritage. In these ways the book, which otherwise has much to recommend it, shows both its own and its writer's age.

In my experience, today's self-identifying 'modern Catholics' tend to be octo- or nonagenarian. For them, to be 'modern' is a badge of honour, a guarantee of their walking unfailingly towards a splendid tomorrow. To their great-grandchildren, meanwhile, the word 'modern' has an old-world ring, a musty perfume of yesteryear. My young brother in the monastery did not scorn 'modernity'. He was too thoughtful for that. But to call someone 'modern' seemed to him faint praise. The notion inspired in him neither confidence nor enthusiasm.

We cannot ascribe this change in sensibility just to a mechanistic pendulum, positing that each new generation rebels against what went before. It is rooted in a decisive, verifiable shift. I think of my parents, who were of Hebblethwaite's generation, more or less. For them, it was axiomatic that the world was getting better every day. The gospel of progress, typical of the post-war years, had formed their view of reality. It had become, to use a fashionable word, their paradigm. One can see why. To have lived through the awfulness of a war that threatened to annihilate all, then to have seen the world reconstitute itself, abetted by undreamt-of progress in science and technology, with so much getting *easier*, gave an intoxicating sense of modernity's saving potential. If we can send people to the moon, read the papers online, and have dishwashers that leave the glasses sparkling, then *anything* is possible!

Confronted with this mindset, I feel positively Jeremian. My gloom, however, is nothing compared to that of today's twenty-year-olds, who could be my children. Often, what they see is a world gone to the dogs, an escalation of mind-blowingly destructive potential made manifest by environmental, political, terroristical, and digital hazards. They see a society in tatters, then look to their elders and ask: How could you let this happen? The question is valid, though often enough is neither heard nor heeded by those to whom it is addressed.

Terms change with the passage of generations. The 'modernity' Peter Hebblethwaite thirty years ago thought to be a synonym for 'reality' has ceased to exist. Cultural historians have pronounced it dead, replaced by *post*-modernity. There are those who claim we now live in *post*-post-modern times. As far as the Church is concerned – the Church we love, which we would serve – this fact is essential. Much Catholic optimism at the time of the council – optimism with regard to engagement with the world, to secular culture, to the scope for dialogue – appears, from the perspective of 2025, touchingly or culpably naive. It is telling that the conciliar constitution that may seem most dated to us is *Gaudium et spes*, qualified as 'Constitutio pastoralis de Ecclesia in mundo huius temporis', a title the official English version rendered, 'Pastoral Constitution on the Church in the *Modern* World', as if the present were destined to remain 'modern' for ever.

When a young Western Catholic today surveys Catholic life in the past half-century, he or she is unlikely – such is my experience – to feel elated. What the young see looking back is not the glorious fulfilment of 'modern' promise, but a swift unravelling: the emptying of seminaries and religious houses, the ageing of congregations, liturgical impoverishment, increasing vagueness in teaching, and the loss of credibility – not least in view of the terrible legacy of sexual abuse. I do not say that this list is objective or exhaustive; I simply say it is what many young Catholics associate with Catholic 'modernity' and its fruits. They are suspicious of the recycling of that era's catchwords: calls for a 'new springtime', for nonjudgemental inclusivism, etc. *Their* concern is to ensure that what they see as a formless Church returns to shape, takes a stand, and reclaims its dignity. We must attend intelligently to this contemporary perspective on the 'modern'. We must seek, 'rooted and built up in [Christ]' (Colossians 2.7), a renewal of fidelity, holiness, coherence, and Catholic zeal unattached to rhetoric that is no longer meaningful.

To dismiss men and women uneasy about 'modern' Catholicism as mindless traditionalists or to accuse them point-blank of being in opposition to the Second Vatican Council is too facile. The council is rarely a subject of controversy, in fact. What raises questions is the way in which it has been applied or instrumentalised. Malaise springs from a sense of loss, issuing in grief. I can relate to such a sense of loss, such grief. During my years as a monastic superior, desiring to work as well as I humanly could to enable a future in a context marked by the opposite of flourishing, I often felt my hands were tied. An abbot, says Saint Benedict, is someone who brings forth from the store things 'both new and old' (see Matthew 13.52). This is hard to do when so much that is old has been labelled redundant and discarded. In terms of liturgy, customs, and observance, most Catholic communities still sail in the wake of a tornado. They are anointed heirs to a project of *aggiornamento*, but the sun has long since set on the *giorno* by which this project was defined. Many of its 'modern' features are fossilised, amiably shaped but lifeless. Confidence in the project has to a large extent gone.

The common ecclesial home energetically stripped and redesigned half a century ago according to fashion, with gadgets then state-of-the-art, has come to feel empty, impractical, and inhospitable to many. One notices design flaws only time can reveal. One looks at the colour schemes and asks, How could anyone have *chosen* this? One wonders, Whatever happened to all the old furniture, all the old books? In terms of Saint Benedict's words, cited above, I often felt, as abbot, like the curator of a collection of fine icons who was not permitted to display them; who must exhibit instead a quantity of finger paintings made at the local school; who was expected to say (and, ideally, think) that the finger paintings were *better*; and all of this, long after most of the children who made them had left school and gone home.

The enterprise of post-conciliar bringing-up-to-date was wholly in view of renewal, conducted with admirable good will, courage, generous hope – and often considerable shortsightedness. In many instances, it has not borne the fruit it was intended to bear. After decades of self-affirmation, it is time to admit this – not to reject an era whose graces and gains are unquestionable, but to no longer rely *a priori* on constant change as the means by which to negotiate crises, to hold fast instead to what endures, to seek stability. 'Gilgamesh, where are you wandering?' These words uttered long ago challenge us. They call for a considered answer, whether we are erring solitarily, in small packs, or in compact *synodos*.

EPOCHAL CHANGE

Pope Francis regularly affirmed, notably in a text calling for 'a paradigm shift, a courageous cultural revolution' in theological reflection, that we are living through 'not merely an epoch of change but a change of epoch'. At a certain level this is self-evident. Ours is a society in flux. It faces constant transformations. Looking back over the period we have considered, we might pinpoint the cultural revolution of 1968, the fall of the Berlin Wall in 1989, the ascendancy of the internet in the 1990s, and the mainstream recognition of global climate change in the 2000s as instances of epochal change, each having occasioned an adjustment of paradigms and cultural turnings-round. We could easily extend the list.

We also find examples of epoch-changing claims that turned out to be premature. Back in the heady days of 2020 and 2021, it was common to speak of COVID-19 as heralding a new epoch. A couple of years later, meanwhile, the virus had in most places been tamed. Where I live it is treated, now, on a par with the common flu. Is there not a risk that our penchant for dividing and subdividing 'epochs' might be a rhetorical concession to the enchantment of a progressivist myth? Is there not in the mindset of exceptionalism regarding our time, as if it necessarily called for measures hitherto unthought-of, an implicit narcissism, a determination to prove to ourselves that we are *special*?

In the context of secular thought, this trend is boring and limiting. The decontextualisation of the present, born of failing or spurned remembrance, can lead to catastrophic misreadings of urgent situations. We ascertain this daily by reading the papers. Authors or coteries of authors who, sure of the unprecedented newness of their insight, cite only themselves, regarding all else as *passé*, effectively aspire to rewrite reality in the first person, be it singular or plural. Such essays may create sensational thrills for a moment or two but are bound for swift oblivion. Reality is so composed that it will not for long let itself be reduced to an abstraction.

When forgetfulness born of progressivist assumptions insinuates itself into the Church's discourse, the stakes are higher. The Christian *kerygma* is premised on the irruption of eternity in time. This implies that essential coordinates are and must remain constant. Think of the acclamation made by the priest at the outset of the Easter Vigil. Inscribing the shape of the cross, the emblem of vanquished death, on the paschal candle, he cries out, 'Christ yesterday and today; the Beginning and the End; the Alpha and the Omega. All time belongs to him, and all ages. To him be glory and power; through every age and for ever.' This capital insight, a source of exultation, is compressed in the Carthusian motto, *Stat crux dum volvitur orbis* (While the world turns, the cross stands firm). It permits us to make a bold claim: Christian engagement with the world has in reality but one decisive paradigm. This paradigm inheres in the fullness of the Church's faith in Christ, defined by the councils and transmitted through a patrimony of theology, liturgy, culture, and charitable action.

When Giovanni Battista Montini became archbishop of Milan in 1954, Pius XII summoned him to an audience. At the end, when Montini rose to leave, the ageing, ailing pope gave him a single counsel: 'Depositum custodi', citing Saint Paul's Second Letter to Timothy (1.14). It is a phrase of substance. The notion of the *depositum fidei* is ancient. It refers to the fullness of faith as contained in Scripture and Tradition. It stands for that without which Christianity ceases to be itself. It is not, though, a static notion. The deposit finds ever new ways of expressing itself. It speaks many languages, assumes different cultural forms. To find its right articulation in the present is the challenge of each generation. What matters is this: not to reduce it to less than itself. Montini succeeded Cardinal Schuster to Milan at a time of turmoil. Of this the pope was more aware than most. He did not tell Montini to be a broken record – to keep mouthing old truths in old ways. He knew Montini – that searching intellect, that sensitive priest – too well. What he told him was: Go and pastor your variegated, scattered flock; find words and gestures they are apt to understand, but don't compromise the truth; have confidence that the deposit entrusted to you will contain the germ of the answers you need to address today's questions; live out of that deposit, dig into it, and dig deeply. This was how Montini explained the pope's words in his inaugural address at Milan, displaying the vast tradition of the

Church as a source of perennial relevance, of perennial newness and originality.

Years later, having become 'the first modern pope', Montini was in anguish at the ease with which Catholics whittled down this great gift, refashioning a grand, sacred reality into a pocket-sized thing. I think for example of the impassioned letter he addressed to the religious orders on 15 August 1966. Aghast at the widespread, head-over-heels rejection of a precious liturgical patrimony, the pope declared himself 'disturbed and saddened'. He asked what the origin was 'of this new way of thinking and this sudden dislike for the past', imploring all 'not to let that spring run dry from which, until the present, they have themselves drunk deep'. Not many attended to the pontiff's words. Convinced, precisely, of constructing a new epoch, most of the people he addressed saw novelty as a non-negotiable imperative. Many of their choicest efforts now resemble ripples in the sea far out towards the horizon.

I began this essay referring to the restlessness of one who lived close to five thousand years ago. I suggested that the fundamental plight of the human condition has not altered much since then. Geologists measure epochs in units of thousands of years. We can learn from them. In terms of essentials, Gilgamesh's epoch is still ours. Sigrid Undset once wrote, 'Customs and conventions change greatly as time passes and man's faith is changed and he thinks differently about many things. But the heart of man changes not at all, at any time.' This is not to belittle man. No, it shows his noble heritage, inviting him to understand himself in the light of all of it. Is it not comforting that we can recognise ourselves in the storm that rode the heart of Gilgamesh? Any earnest effort of human self-understanding must apply a hermeneutic of continuity.

That seems to me self-evident. In a Christian context, it becomes axiomatic, a necessary consequence of the Incarnation of the Word.

In the *Epic of Gilgamesh*, the sun god Shamash asks the king of Uruk, 'Where are you wandering?' The Church's task is to pose that question to the women and men of our time, proposing a direction. The *Epic of Gilgamesh* took shape at the time which yields primordial evidence of a God at once revealed and concealed by an ineffable name, the *Tetragrammaton*. Uruk was not far from Ur of the Chaldees, where Abram heard the call, 'Go from your country and your kindred and your father's house to the land that I will show you' (Genesis 12.1). This call remains for us exemplary, an invitation to set out as pilgrims. Abram, though, was not summoned out of Ur for the journey's sake, but to travel to a land that would be for him, and for his children, *home*. He walked up and down it, claiming it for the Lord. He dug wells there to benefit Isaac, his son, and his offspring. Let us look briefly into those wells.

We may set out from the twenty-sixth chapter of the book of Genesis. It tells of how Isaac, fleeing a famine, travelled southwest to Gerar, south of Gaza, to sojourn with Abimelech, king of the Philistines. Contrary to what it had been reasonable to expect, he prospered in exile, obtaining flocks and herds. 'The Philistines envied him'. So what did they do? They conducted the sabotage to which nomadic herdsmen were most vulnerable. They 'stopped up and filled with earth all the wells that [Isaac's] father's servants had dug in the days of his father Abraham'.

Isaac was not fatally set back. Why not? He remembered where the wells were. '[He] dug again the wells of water that had been dug in the days of his father Abraham . . . and he gave them the names that his father had given them.' He then dug a series of new wells.

That done, one night at Beersheba, the Lord appeared to him and said: 'I am the God of your father Abraham; do not be afraid, for I am with you and will bless you and make your offspring numerous.' Isaac built an altar there in commemoration; he pitched his tent; and for good measure, he dug yet another well.

I love Origen's take on this story. His eagle eye saw the unfolding of events as a parable for the life of faith. In Isaac, he saw a type of Christ. 'This Isaac, then, our Saviour, on entering [our] vale of Gerar, first of all wished to dig out the wells once dug by the servants of his father, renewing the wells of the law and prophets, which Philistines had filled with earth." To Origen, the 'earth' stopping the wells was a too earthly view that blocked the gushing of living water, quenching the Spirit (see 1 Thessalonians 5.19). To move towards the fulfilment of God's promise, it is needful first to look back, to turn *ad fontes*, as Vatican II taught, and take advantage of past blessings.

The Genesis account then talks of new wells. Isaac dug them as he continued on his path, following God's guidance, to provide for new circumstances as they arose. Jesus, whom Isaac prefigures, likewise dug. Origen delights in the fact that Isaac's third well, the work of his hands, was called *Rehoboth*, which means 'broadness'. 'For truly', he says, 'Isaac has now extended himself and caused his name to be broad over all the earth, filling it with the name of the Trinity.' The new Isaac reveals the extent of the mystery of God in a definitive way. From this revelation, evangelists of all times, including ours, receive their mission: to carry the saving name of Jesus to the ends of the earth, digging wells in his name as they go.

Origen, never content with the surface of things, saw a third level of meaning in Isaac's digging by letting it resound within a story told in the fourth chapter of John. Talking with the Samaritan woman, Christ uses work connected with a village well to explain spiritual realities: 'Those who drink of the water that I will give them will never be thirsty. The water that I will give will become in them a spring of water gushing up to eternal life' (John 4.14). Origen is in no doubt: Here is the key that unlocks the ancient enterprise of Isaac. 'The Word of God is present among us', he says, 'and this is what he is now about: from the soul of each one of you he wishes to dig out accumulated earth to open your wellspring. For the well is *within you*, it does not issue from elsewhere, even as the kingdom of God is within'. In each of us the new Isaac labours, clearing out our pretensions and shabby attachments, eager to make our souls 'broad'. He would free of sludge the wellspring we carry so that, from a trickle, it will rise into a sanctifying fountain.

CONCLUSION

Sometimes I ask myself what historians five hundred years hence will highlight when they analyse the history of the Church in the late twentieth and early twenty-first centuries. Will they see it as the hinge on which epochs turned, an age defined by 'the council' or 'the synod', a time of renewal and great innovation? Perhaps. But again, perhaps not. What we consider gigantic enterprise *hic et nunc*, because we identify ourselves with it, is not necessarily what leaves a lasting mark on the historical process. Decisive influences tend to be subtler. Perhaps the future's historians, looking back at us, will highlight not the great moving and shaking, but rather certain reconquests from tradition that stand for the unblocking of wells. It is not implausible, for instance, that the page and a half dedicated to our time in a twenty-sixth-century history of the

Church might begin with the observation, 'This was the period that rediscovered Origen', pointing less to events, and more to intuitions preparing and underpinning a spiritual and intellectual movement whose lasting impact we are yet unfit to gauge. The example of Gilgamesh teaches us that monuments and conquests, for making a lot of noise, are perishable. What abides is of a different order. What abides pertains to the epoch-defying storm of the human heart and to the resilience of truly meaningful words. To gather such words, to let them echo in the heart and to scrutinise them with the mind, is man's prerogative and duty. We need, to go about that duty, a standard of evaluation. Scripture chronicles the growing consciousness of a single, God-given Word that makes sense of and orders all other words. In the fullness of time, this Word became flesh. It revealed a face and a name at which every knee shall bend, 'in heaven and on earth and under the earth' (Philippians 2.10). The last and lasting Word, we are given to intuit, transcends the vast multitude of words uttered in time, drawing these towards an intelligible whole whose real finality is not discourse but praise, in a cosmic communion of homage.

One of Origen's sermons on Exodus offers an account of the bestowal of manna in the wilderness. The Lord told the people, 'In the morning you shall have your fill of bread' (Exodus 16.12). Origen read that verse as pointing towards Christ the Morning Star, come to make all things new. The edition of Origen's sermons in the collection *Sources chrétiennes* was presented by Father Henri de Lubac just after the Second World War, in the summer of 1947. The learned Jesuit permitted himself, at this point, an expostulation by way of a footnote. Breaking with the austere conventions of scholarly apparatus, he wrote of the morning manna:

To Origen Christ restores to an ageing world perpetual youth. Thus is conveyed the considered sentiment of gladness that bore up the first Christian communities, conscious, at once, of being heirs to a most ancient tradition and yet of embodying a new world. It still depends on the Christian of today whether Christianity will appear to all as the world's youth and its hope.

We shall rise to this challenge if we stay rooted in Christ, *Lumen gentium*; if we live and work 'through him, with him, and in him', letting him be the paradigm defining all our aspirations. Doing so, we may find that our current crises do in fact have much in common with crises of the past. In an encyclical dated 1 November 1914, as the world was sinking into a spiral of self-destruction, Pope Benedict XV declared his conviction that the only way to confront with Christian integrity the end of civilisation was a determined focus on Christ's salvific action, letting the world's processes be explained by it, not *vice versa*. The guiding light for such cataclysmic times, said the pontiff, was the adage *Non nova, sed noviter* (Not new things, but in a new way). It may be neither opportune nor necessary to come up with new things constantly; we must first use and apply what has been given us in new ways, trustfully reading ourselves into a providential context in which 'a thousand years are like one day' (2 Peter 3.8).

The world about us now is swept away by a rhythm increasingly resembling that of a *danse macabre*. Its multiple voices shout each other out in often fearful cacophony. There is no established score, no one conducting. We need to set another pace, even if it incurs the rage of the fast-whirling crowds. We need to listen out for the one perfect, penetrating pitch by which alone our instruments may be symphonically tuned. The fourteenth-century mystic Jan van Ruusbroec envisaged Christ as the conductor of a universal symphony able to incorporate into itself the groaning of creation as it waits in pangs of childbirth for the full redemption of the sons of God. In that symphony, the voices of our time resound in harmony with those of Abraham and Gilgamesh. To keep that hope-filled, significant music alive is the Church's obligation, mission, and sublime privilege.

2

Can Literature Save Lives?

In a book from 1947, *If This Is a Man*, a careful account of an experience of Auschwitz, the Italian pharmacist Primo Levi reflects on the concentration camp's significance as an anthropological phenomenon. In the book there is an unforgettable chapter entitled 'The Canto of Odysseus'. It tells of a day on which Levi was given an unusual commission. He was commandeered out to fetch that day's food ration, a cauldron of watery soup, for his company. Designating him for this task was Jean, a twenty-four-year-old from Alsace. Jean was a rare bird in Auschwitz. He had risen in the hierarchy of prisoners; he was on good terms with the brutal guards. But he was not himself brutalised. We are told there was a gentleness about him. He was *kind*.

When Levi started scurrying along, Jean said, 'We have time.' All at once it was possible to look around, to rediscover oneself as a subject capable of thought, observation, and emotion. They saw 'the Carpathians covered in snow'. 'I breathed in the fresh air', writes Levi, 'I felt unusually light-hearted.' The two of them spoke about where they came from, about their studies, about books they had read. They told one another about their mothers. Jean, who spoke fluent French and German, said he would very much like to learn Italian. Levi exclaimed, 'I can teach you!' They would have to begin at once. Who knew when they would again be on their own, able to talk freely? Who knew whether they would even still be alive the next day?

That is when it happened. Spontaneously, out of long-forgotten depths, Dante arose in Levi's remembrance. He had studied him at school, as an obligatory subject, without much enthusiasm. A seed, though, had been sown.

It was absurd; Primo Levi could see that quite clearly. Was he to introduce his mother tongue there in the camp, dressed in filthy rags, with perhaps half an hour at disposal, on the basis of one of world literature's chiefest masterpieces? Yes, that was exactly what he was going to do. Frenetically, he started explaining what the *Divine Comedy* represents, what the roles of Virgil and Beatrice stand for, the peculiar sense one has of constantly discovering within this venerable text something *new*. Jean, writes Levi, listened with great attention. Levi began to recite from memory. The passage he instantly recalled was from the twenty-sixth canto of the *Inferno*. It is where Dante meets Odysseus, who, enclosed in an eternally ardent flame, recounts his journey into the unknown after the end of the Trojan War. Having reached home, reunited with Ithaca, no bond could keep him from seeking what he yearned for, which eclipsed the prospect of calm retirement: He wished to experience the world the way it is, in order, as he says, 'a divenir del mondo esperto' (to become 'an expert' of the world). Let us remember that to be an 'expert' is to have *experientia*, to have lived through that which one attempts to convey.

Having recited for a while, Levi made a pause to try to translate and explain. It was 'disastrous', he affirms – 'poor Dante, and poor French', French being the language into which he was trying to paraphrase. Jean, meanwhile, was avid for more. He asked Levi to continue: 'What happens next?' Suddenly Levi found himself disconsolate. He realised what holes there were in his remembering. Only fragments could be found, scattered pieces of a mosaic that did not sufficiently enable one to see the whole picture. Jean did not care. He was pleased to contemplate these details, the individual polished *tessere* Levi was able to display. He drew the text out from his friend.

In that way it was given him to hear words that peculiarly touched them right where they were. In the canto, Odysseus describes the Pillars of Hercules by Gibraltar, promontories raised by the gods 'that none should prove so hard / To venture the unchartered distances' – into a sea alive with unknown menace. The two prisoners realised together, silently, that that was precisely where they were: out on the open, terrible sea. A further Dantean line, extracted from Levi's memory store, sounded poignantly:

> *Considerate la vostra semenza:*
> *Fatti non foste a viver come bruti,*
> *Ma per seguir virtute e conoscenza.*

> Consider your provenance; you were not made
> To live like beasts; you were made
> to follow after virtue and knowledge.

It was, Levi writes, 'as if I was hearing [the words] for the first time, like the blast of a trumpet, like the very voice of God. For a moment I forgot who I was and where I was.'

Jean asked him to repeat the stanza: 'How good [Jean] is, aware that it is doing me good. Or perhaps something more is at stake, perhaps, despite the wan translation, despite the pedestrian, rushed commentary, he has received the message, he has felt that it has to do with him, that it has to do with all men who toil, and with us in particular; and that it has to do with us two who dare to reason of these things with the poles for the soup on our shoulders'.

Walking along in this singular tandem, yoked to the cauldron, Levi evoked for Jean, through Dante, one commanding image after another: the mountain peaks Odysseus saw, which with aching sweetness recalled the mountains surrounding his home town of Turin; the tear-drenched earth, 'terra lagrimosa', that sadly presented the camp itself; then Odysseus's description of his boat's capsizing beyond the pillars, at the end of the earth, its prow headed downward, following 'another's [destiny's, Neptune's] good pleasure' until the waters closed over it for ever. It was immense, this lucid, realistic, poetic expression of an experience that otherwise spelled utter senselessness. Levi asks: Might the purpose of our being here today be that we entertain this intuition, ascertain this possibility of articulation? The very possibility that purpose might exist rekindled in him a courage he had thought quite gone.

LAYERS OF SIGNIFICANCE

Levi's narrative is enacted at several different levels at once. The question shaping the book is: What is a human being? With this as our point of departure, let us consider what goes on in the text.

The first thing we notice touches the level of psychology: Levi is affirmed in his humanity by owning himself as a bearer of culture. The realisation does him good. The camp's Kommando might take away his name and history, reduce his identity to a number tattooed in blue ink on his wrist. He remains nonetheless a man possessed of Dante. He carries within a noble heritage of which no earthly power can deprive him. To see this is to reappropriate dignity. Levi's remembrance of the *Inferno* represents the first stage of a kind of personal awakening.

A further dimension of significance opens when he shares what he carries with another. Jean gives Primo breathing space by proposing their joint mission; yet they remain within the all-embracing material and mental enclosure of the camp. On their way to the soup kitchen, they meet people who ruthlessly recall them to where they are: Rudi the Blockführer, Frenkel the snitch. The cauldron-bearers point them out to one another by means of meaningful glances and lapidary whispered remarks. The camp is a perfectly introverted system. The world beyond the barbed-wire fence seems as remote as Orion in the night sky. This was the method of Auschwitz. The prisoners were not supposed to believe or recall that life exists elsewhere. Dante enabled a liberating subversion. The encounter with his text allowed Primo and Jean to rise above totalitarian restriction, to let their minds soar in fellowship. In the midst of degradation, Primo discovered that he still had something to *give*. Jean had the humane ability to *receive*. For a brief moment, they could enact the roles of host and guest to one another. This gracious relationship is basic to the ancient story of Odysseus. Perhaps no other relationship lends human dignity clearer expression. The conversation about Dante thus acquires a political dimension, if we think of politics as the construction of society. The exchange between Primo and Jean stands for constructive rebellion in its most magnanimous form.

I would like to point out a third aspect of this exchange. It seems to me the most important of all. It inaugurates a new way of interpreting or understanding extreme experience. Should we want to attach a Greek-sounding label to this aspect too (in line with the psychological and political), we might call it hermeneutic. The *Divine Comedy* is not merely a venerable book. It is a book that spells out the vocation and role of man in time and eternity. It tells us what the drama of life is about.

There is little sentimental comfort in Dante's message. Don't forget, the canto of Odysseus belongs to that part of the *Comedy* that bears the name *Inferno*. The song issues from eternally inextinguishable fire. But is it not the case that we, when we are really hurting, do not primarily seek release, but recognition? We want someone else to *acknowledge* that we suffer without necessarily expecting that he or she will take our pain away. Dante's vision of eternity frames in words an experience that otherwise appears chaotic and absurd, unattached to any sense-bearing structure.

Even the terrible final verse about Odysseus's sinking ship contributes to a scenario of realism and factuality: *This* is life now. To relinquish a vision of what life should, could, or might have been for a vision that recognises life the way it is, forfeiting illusion for the sake of reality, rekindles authority, lets us take possession of life as subjects. We are no longer hapless, victimised objects of things that happen. We find ourselves endowed with positive selfhood, and thus with powers of agency. To have hollowed out in oneself, thanks to transmitted insight, a space for such drastic recognition is to be equipped with a reservoir of inner strength. One is armed to confront the real, even when it is awful.

RESONANCE AND RECOGNITION

I set out from a question: Can literature save lives? I submit that yes, it can. Of course, there is literature and *literature*. I think of an interview Nadia Boulanger gave at the end of the 1970s, when she was about ninety years old and blind. Throughout a long life, she had taught composition, counterpoint, and other fundamental subjects at the Paris Conservatoire. A whole generation of composers from Bernstein to Piazzolla attended her rigorous school. She is remembered as a consummate, stern pedagogue. Yet she had herself composed as a young woman. In the interview, Bruno Monsaingeon asks her why on earth she gave it up. The *grande dame* answered firmly, 'Because I saw that my music was useless, *une musique inutile*'. It was lovely, academic, well thought-out, but did not contribute anything *new*. For that reason she found no joy in it and decided to devote her life instead to the transmission of an essential heritage.

We could apply these same criteria to literature. There are piles of books we might read with pleasure and profit in bed, on the train, on the beach, or as an audiobook in a traffic jam, but they will leave no lasting mark on us. There is nothing wrong with such reading; on the contrary. But it is hardly remembrance of *The Famous Five* that will sustain us in a crisis. These days we are obsessively careful to nurture our bodies responsibly and well. We take magnesium, cod-liver oil, and Vitamin D; we reinforce our bones, mind our iron levels, eat all sorts of oriental roots to prevent calcification. Do we in like proportion nurture our inner lives? In an ardent poem from 1936 addressed 'To Youth', the Norwegian poet Nordahl Grieg pointed towards the 'gliding thread of grenades' that were set to rend the cultural and social order of Europe. He exclaimed, 'Stop their deathward drift / Stop them with spirit'. It is an attractive imperative. It is also very demanding. We are so composed and conditioned that most of us are naturally less full of 'spirit' than of hot air. Spirit must be sought out, received, nourished, shared. We must accustom ourselves to absorbing spiritual food as something essential.

A few years ago, I read the diary of Nicu Steinhardt, a Jewish Romanian thinker arrested by the Securitate in 1962, then kept incarcerated for years. The fact that he called his diary secretly written up *The Journal of Joy* says much about his stamina and stature. Let me cite a remark he made concerning one of his first days in jail, back in February 1962: 'From day one I find an enormous thirst for poetry among my cellmates. The most satisfying, inexhaustible way of passing time in prison is to learn poetry by heart. Blessed are those who know poetry! The prisoner who knows many poems by heart is fortunate. He can spend many hours in a discreet and dignified way. . . . Father Faria knew what he was doing when, in order to ready himself for the isle of Montecristo, he memorised his library'.

Steinhardt sketches a portrait of one of the men with whom he shared a cell. This man, called Harald Sigmund, was a Lutheran pastor from Brașov, learned in poetry. He had translated Rainer Maria Rilke into Romanian. He had made the poet's words his own and recited them, Steinhardt says, wonderfully. In a striking passage, Steinhardt describes Sigmund's contribution to the life of the prison cell:

> He spontaneously turned out to represent a miracle that rarely arises in a convict but that, when we meet it, allows us to know what joy is: he was a courageous, proud, indomitable man, as courteous as if he had found himself in the drawing room of the duke of Conti, . . . always smiling and noble, like the models in the painting of Van Loo; always benevolent, never sullen or taciturn; constantly ready and willing to learn all new things, to converse, listen, and speak, to pass on all he himself knows: He is a gentleman, an aristocrat, a hero.

Harald Sigmund was more, of course, than just a man of literature. He was a man of faith, a man who embodied life in Christ; yet literature had formed him and made him so peculiarly beneficial for others. By means of the heritage he carried, he brought, like Levi in Auschwitz, *humanity* into the dank, hopeless spaces of captivity; he brought strength that was at once psychologically, politically, and hermeneutically liberating. In this way, he kindled a spark of spirit also in others. Left to themselves, they would have languished and sunk into darkness. He reminded them of what a human being *can* be even in inhuman circumstances.

At this point you may be getting impatient and think: This is all very well and good, but nonetheless highfalutin snobbery – fine for folks who find themselves in a cell where the prisoners all have doctorates and, back in the comfort of their homes, listen to the Brandenburg Concertos each Sunday after breakfast, but out of reach for ordinary people. I would disagree with such an objection. I think we are talking about something pan-human, of universal relevance. I consider it a vital task (and a Christian, Catholic task) here and now to counter the stupid tendency that would make of culture a luxury for the elites while presuming that the one truly unifying medium for our times is TikTok.

I can present a witness in support of my case. I do not know her name. No one does. The memorial I have of her outlines an anonymous profile; yet it is so compelling, so pregnant with life, that one cannot, once one has perceived it, ever forget it. We find this memorial in the introduction to Anna Akhmatova's *Requiem*, a cycle of poems completed in 1957. It treats of the years of the great terror from 1935 to 1940. Akhmatova, who had in her youth been a comet in Russia's literary firmament, had already for years been a societal outcast. Her husband, Nikolay Gumilyov, had been executed as an enemy of the state in 1921. In the 30s, her son, Lev, sat behind bars in Leningrad as a political prisoner. Day after day, Akhmatova stood with countless other mothers before the prison gate who hoped to deliver, quite simply, a letter, a parcel of food, warm socks, or underwear to a beloved husband, father, son, or friend on the other side of the wall.

Minimalistically, but with primeval, maternal passion, she conjures up the atmosphere in a vignette entitled 'In lieu of a foreword':

> In the terrible years of the Yezhov terror [Nikolay Yezhov, you will remember, was from 1936 head of the NKVD, the predecessor of the KGB, where Russia's current president acquired work experience], I spent seventeen months in the prison lines of Leningrad. Once, someone 'recognised' me. Then a woman with bluish lips standing behind me, who, of course, had never heard me called by name before, woke up from the stupor to which everyone had succumbed and whispered in my ear (everyone spoke in whispers there): 'Can you describe this?' And I

answered, 'Yes, I can'. Then something that looked like a smile passed over what had once been her face'.

I first heard this text read aloud on Norwegian television. I was a teenager. The programme covered the launch of a recently published volume of Akhmatova's poems in translation. The words instantly became a part of me; since then, this woman with blue lips has belonged to my life. By a stroke of her pen, Akhmatova made her immortal. The woman was no intellectual. Akhmatova's name would probably have meant little to her. What mattered to her was this: to know that there stood, in among the other *babushkas*, a poet able to express in words a grief she herself was unable to name. This discovery restored, for a moment, movement and personality to her petrified mask: 'Something that looked like a smile passed over what had once been her face.'

'NOT BORN FOR DEATH'

I have spoken of the power of words, of letters, in conditions we, thank God, are unlikely to know and, please God, shall never know. Extreme circumstances confer extreme lucidity; crises clarify. They make it easier to see what counts and what does not. By way of conclusion, however, I should like to say something of the life-giving power of literature in the simple drab of everyday life. Here, too, we can entertain moments of revelation when beauty and sense – or the *possibility* of beauty and sense – pierce our sensibility through the agency of words.

We find testimony to such revelation in Janet Frame's autobiography *An Angel at My Table*, a work whose profundity does not appear in Jane Campion's movie adaptation, bearing the same name, from 1990. Frame was one of New Zealand's most notable authors in the twentieth century. She grew up endowed with tremendous giftedness of soul in material poverty. Her inner life was so strong, so compelling, that she often found herself at cross-purposes with so-called normal life. She became known for her otherness: 'Jane is so different.' The people around her could only conceive of such difference as an indication of sickness.

Frame was declared schizophrenic. From the mid-1940s she was kept in institutions, 'treated' with electroconvulsive therapy. By a hair's breadth, she avoided lobotomisation. It happened that a book she had written, *The Lagoon*, won a literary prize. The hospital's director had seen a note about this in the paper. He came to her and declared, with Olympian authority, 'I've decided that you should stay as you are.' Frame was allowed to start life again on new terms. Having gone through a thorough course of psychoanalysis in London, she was declared well: the specialist concluded that she was not in fact schizophrenic and never had been. She was simply a woman of singular sensibility struggling to find her place in the world.

It is useful to be reminded that this sort of thing *can* happen: that which one day is promoted as a philanthropically motivated, scientifically grounded diagnosis leading into identity-changing surgery *can*, the next day, be found to be unreal – a hair-raising projection.

Literature let Frame find a foothold. She gradually dared to believe that truth sought and found through reading and writing was not necessarily a form of escapism, but could convey real insight. I have often thought it would be fruitful to conduct a parallel reading of Frame and the Norwegian author Tarjei Vesaas, best known in the English-speaking world for his novel *The Birds*, serially nominated for the Nobel Prize from the end of World War II onward, whose wife Halldis, incidentally, co-translated Anna Akhmatova. Both writers draw with intelligence and sympathy the contours of liminal human experience that a less informed, less patient perspective inclines to declare pathological, to be medicalised away. But such a comparative reading would be work for another day.

Here, I wish to focus on a particular incident in Janet Frame's book, the story of an important encounter: her reunion with Poppy. The two had known one another since they were girls. Poppy 'had lank brown hair, an ugly face with a wide red mouth, and her father whipped her with a narrow machine belt, which made cuts in her skin.' Poppy had made the world her own. She knew the name of every plant in the field; she knew how to cure warts; she knew about and had the fierce audacity to name the processes of reproduction. In one of her father's old beer barrels, she kept a copy of *Grimms' Fairy Tales*. The Brothers Grimm gave the girls a common language. 'Suddenly', writes Frame, 'the world of living and the world of reading linked in a way I had not noticed before. . . . Grimms' Fairy Tales was everybody's story seen in a special way, with something new added to the ordinary rules of observation' – a transfigured perspective, we might say, which let Janet and Poppy interpret their lives in a novel way. Their conversation, though, came to an abrupt end. The girls' families thought the two of them were not good for one another. They were forbidden to meet and obeyed – as one did at that time, in that environment – blindly.

Ten or twelve years later, they met again at a high school. Frame's old friend turned out to be taking a commercial course. The wild, knowing, sensual Poppy had morphed into a sensible maiden in a grey skirt. 'I am doing shorthand, typing, double-entry bookkeeping', she proclaimed, as if such catastrophic competence pointed towards an abyss. 'There was a resigned air, a seriousness about our meeting. We could have been two soldiers on a battlefield, exchanging notes about our possibility of survival'. Frame notes, 'The word commercial aroused so much horror in me that I could scarcely believe in Poppy's survival.'

It was in many ways a cold meeting. What was there to be said? Only when they were about to part did something happen. Poppy revived, became recognisable. She told Jane she was studying Keats' 'Ode to a Nightingale'. The poem featured in an anthology called *Mount Helicon* intended to confer on tomorrow's executive secretaries a varnish of sophistication. '"We have to learn some verses", Poppy said, beginning to recite', sharing the entire penultimate stanza:

> Thou wast not born for death, immortal Bird!
>   No hungry generations tread thee down;
> The voice I hear this passing night was heard
>   In ancient days by emperor and clown:
> Perhaps the self-same song that found a path
>   Through the sad heart of Ruth, when,
> sick for home,
>   She stood in tears amid the alien corn;
>   The same that oft-times hath
> Charm'd magic casements, opening on the foam
>   Of perilous seas, in faery lands forlorn.

Frame listened with astonishment and reverence. Poppy's voice sounded 'with passionate intimacy, as if the poem were directly related to her, as if it were a milestone in her own life'. There was something so pathetic in the motif of forlornness, as if anything worth striving for were already consigned to the past. The despair of the verse 'No hungry generations tread thee down' poured forth from Poppy 'like a cry of panic'. The poem represented a stark contrast to the acquired persona of the young woman lined up with her bookkeeping and stenography. Yet it was entirely hers. Poppy communicated it by way of a secret handshake, as if she said, I have not forgotten, I will not vanish, even if life blots me out. The two never met again. Frame later learned that Poppy had left the school that same year, 'soon married and settled in one of the coastal towns of Otago'.

Who knows what became of Poppy? Hardly a poet. But perhaps some kind of artist all the same, even if her life turned into a battle for existence. Something had been awakened in her early enough, insight making it possible to frame even unfulfilled longing in words. What we can name or conceptualise in an image, we can live with. Indeed, we can integrate it into the poetry that constitutes our life according to Saint Paul's magnificent statement in Ephesians (2.10): [Θεοῦ] γὰρ ἐσμεν ποίημα. This line is conventionally translated 'We are God's handiwork', but we might responsibly render it 'We are God's poem', as if each element of our existence were a phrase, a line, a letter, or just a comma, perhaps, destined for integration into a meaningful statement lovely in its providential perfection.

Ours is a time of loneliness. One year before I left Great Britain, the government appointed a Minister for Loneliness. A department of state was thought to be required. Other countries may well think the same. We are conscious of serious issues in mental health, especially among the young.

I shall not presume to present some sort of universal diagnosis. May God preserve us now and always from clerical quackery. I am bound by my office, though, to attempt to understand a social crisis from a perspective of spirituality and faith. I believe that the spiritual life of a human being is substantial and definitive, unfolding in fine-tuned balance with our psychological life. I dare, then, to make this affirmation: I submit that existential superficiality, conceptual impoverishment, and a want of words are serious issues with an impact on public health in our time. We experience deeply, we perceive and feel deeply; that is simply the way we are. But fewer and fewer people have words adequate to name the depths they experience, perceive, and feel. That leaves them vulnerable to movements and individuals which hand out banal and simplifying identity-designating tags, with convenient offers of relabelling. In order to live, to survive, and to thrive we need to practise the art of living consciously at a certain depth, there to confront ourselves and others, plumbing the deep meaning of our joy *and* pain.

As a Christian I believe, of course, that the meaning of life has a face, bears a name. The book we simply call Scripture alone provides definitive answers. Such is my belief. But experience shows that Scripture can be a difficult book to approach; one has to be rooted in one's true humanity *first*. In this respect, poetry and literature can represent a propaedeutic stage. Malcolm X reached this conclusion when, in the 40s, he served a prison sentence that transformed him from a young criminal into an activist for human rights. 'I'm a real bug for poetry', he wrote to his brother on 4 February 1949.

'When you think back over all of our past lives, only poetry could best fit into the vast emptiness created by men.'

If literature equips us to recognise and name emptiness, it is also likely to let us discover that empty resonance does not have the last word. A living, life-giving Word can rise out of the night of felt extinction. When that happens, literature can save lives, resurrect hope, perhaps even turn into a vehicle of salvation.

3

The Body at Prayer

I was a doctoral student when a friend passed on to me a second-hand copy of a book by the Belgian Benedictine Jean Déchanet, a monk of Saint-André de Bruges. Déchanet, born in 1906, was known to me as a medieval scholar. His work on William of Saint-Thierry, the chief intellectual among the twelfth-century school of Cistercian Fathers, has defined much modern reception of that attractive, subtle thinker. Déchanet established a Latin edition of William's *Golden Epistle*, which he also translated. Given this backdrop, I was puzzled by the title and content of the book given me. In French it was published in 1956, complete with an imprimatur, as *La Voie du silence: Yoga pour chrétien*. The English version produced four years later by Harper in New York was titled more straightforwardly *Christian Yoga*.

So was this austere examiner of manuscripts, a man seemingly at home in a monastic environment *à la* Eco's *The Name of the Rose*, at the same time some kind of hippie, drawn like the Beatles by the mystique and stillness of the fragrant Orient?

Father Déchanet countered this predictable objection in his

preface to the third edition of *La Voie du silence*, out in 1963 after the book had sold tens of thousands of copies. Not only, he pointed out, was his interest in yoga not at odds with his study of the medieval theologian. It was a consequence of such engagement. He wrote,

> I was led to Yoga by William of Saint-Thierry. For twenty years I lived under the aegis and influence of his living psychology, which in turn had been taken and adapted from Origen (himself an Oriental). My chief concern has been to ensure that in me there should exist that balance of *anima, animus* and *spiritus* which he makes the precondition . . . of the unfolding in man of the grace of our Lord, and of the transition from the image (the mark of which is clearly set on these 'three') to divine resemblance. The creature, cut off from God by sin and divided, moreover, within himself, cannot entertain the hope of finding his Creator or his lost intimacy with him otherwise than by first of all making use of the grace of Christ the Redeemer and of his power and example, in order to fashion himself anew in the image of God, to re-establish unity in himself, and to rediscover the natural order in the order of charity.

William's position as retold by Déchanet instances a soaring intuition that informed much twelfth-century enterprise as European Christians increasingly sensed the potential nobility of embodied human nature. Of course, this intuition was not universally shared. It struggled, like any new life, to be born. By way of example, Helen Waddell amiably contrasts the perception of Bernard of Clairvaux with that of his younger contemporary, the philosopher Bernard

Sylvestris, herald of a catholic synthesis accomplished in the next, thirteenth century, which produced persons and monuments that still hold out to us a measure of what we think of as 'humane'. Waddell calls this synthesis a 'Truce of God', a reconciliation that ended at last an age-old war between the spirit and the flesh, 'even as the Last Judgement of the Western rose-window in Chartres melts into "heaven's own colour, blue".' Where Bernard of Clairvaux had spoken of 'the dungheap of the flesh', she notes, Bernard Sylvestris saw in the union of flesh and spirit 'a discipline that made for greatness, and the body itself a not ignoble hospice for the pilgrim soul.'

The Cistercian Bernard, harsh in his quips, treated his own flesh harshly. Excessive mortification forced him early in his abbacy to take a time of monastic sick-leave in a hermitage near Clairvaux. That was where William of Saint-Thierry, still a Benedictine, first met him in 1118. The two became firm friends. It is plausible that they talked even then of the body's status in man's spiritual quest. William harboured the conviction that our body is intrinsic to who we *are*, constituting not just a tent to shelter our sojourn in this vale of tears but an intentionally imaged reality susceptible of godlikeness. William's tripartite anthropology, to which Déchanet refers, conceives of the human being as a composite of physicality, soul-reason, and spirit. These distinctions shape *The Golden Epistle*'s three-part division, taking us from Animal Man (the human being considered in its embodiment), through Rational Man (accounting for man's intellective faculties), to Spiritual Man (envisaging transformation by grace), not as if these were successive scores to be rehearsed, one surpassing the other, but as a perfectly balanced polyphonic motet.

Déchanet was not content to expound this anthropology in

monographs. He wanted, he says, 'to ensure that in me there should exist that balance of *anima, animus* and *spiritus*'. He was a monk, pursuing theology as part of the overall quest on which he had staked his life, to behold what Saint Benedict calls 'the deifying light' and to be transformed, remade by it. Déchanet's personal circumstances raised the stakes. He says he had been 'an invalid from childhood on' – suffering cruelly from epilepsy – 'but when I was about forty, I was providentially cured, and felt a consuming urge to live'. The French original speaks of 'un impérieux besoin de vivre', a *need* entertained as an imperative, as if in intimate response to an oracle like that addressed to Ezekiel in the parable of the unsalted, unswaddled infant whom the Lord picks up and raises high: 'I passed by you, and saw you flailing about in your blood. As you lay in your blood, I said to you, "Live!"' (16.6).

I was stirred by Déchanet's passage when I read it as a young man. I also wanted, *needed* to live. I still find his text a compelling statement of Christian purpose. That is not, though, my reason for invoking it today. I want instead to point to a self-evident but still curious paradox: When this cultured Belgian Benedictine, avid for life in his fifth decade – having taught himself to swim at forty-two, loosening up his limbs – sought an effective tool with which to *spiritualise* his body in pursuit of his *animus*'s harmonious union with *anima* and *spiritus*, he spontaneously looked towards yoga, rehearsing asanas after vigils in his cell before an open window.

Yoga, of course, was in the air. Paramahansa Yogananda had published his *Autobiography of a Yogi* in 1946 after a quarter-century of energetic teaching in the United States. Millions read, and still read, this book. Steve Jobs had copies handed out to all those who attended his own memorial service at Stanford on 16 October 2011, a posthumous benefaction. In the 1950s, the West encountered, too, the hugely influential teachings of B. K. S. Iyengar, whose chief ambassador was the violinist Yehudi Menuhin. Menuhin maintained that the practice of yoga had liberated his playing. He called Iyengar 'my best violin teacher'. Yogananda and Iyengar were but two high-profile proponents of a more general trend eliciting in Boston, London, and Paris a massive, enchanted response. Monks, like everyone else, became curious. Father Bede Griffiths practised yoga at Farnborough in the years following World War II and left for India in 1955, as did Father Francis Acharya, a Trappist of Scourmont who founded Kurisumala. Father Jules Monchanin, a diocesan priest with monastic aspirations, had lived in India since 1939 and was joined there in 1948 by Father Henri Le Saux of Kergonan, later known throughout the world as Abhishiktananda.

These Catholic clerics were intelligent and articulate. Their reports from the spiritual front line, thought by many to lie in the Far East, trickled into the remotest cloisters, setting off a wave of interest, enquiry, and experimentation. Déchanet may have practised 'The Serpent', 'The Dolphin', 'The Folded Leaf', and other yogic postures in solitude at Saint André, but all over Europe, monks and nuns, not to mention countless lay people, were doing the same. The lasting impact of this movement is obvious: so-called 'Christian Yoga' is a mainstream phenomenon now.

I have sketched an aspirational movement that began gently in Europe and the US after the First World War, picked up momentum after the Second, then became a tidal wave in the 1960s, corresponding to the yearning of people in a fast-moving, ever more materialist West truly to inhabit their bodies and to realise a deeply felt hunch that their physical self is a reliable bearer of meaning.

Menuhin wrote in a foreword to Iyengar's book *Light on Yoga* in 1980: 'Reduced to our own body, our first instrument, we learn to play it, drawing from it maximum resonance and harmony. With unflagging patience we refine and animate every cell, . . . unlocking and liberating capacities otherwise condemned to frustration and death.'

This purpose of self-realisation acquires special poignancy in a Christian optic, which holds that the human being is made, made *entirely*, in the image of God. One can see how a sincere and thoughtful Christian like Father Déchanet would pursue it with contemplative conviction, giving rise to a school of practice.

Having established as much, let us leave our Christian yogis distended in a posture of repose while we turn our minds to a simultaneous and in many ways parallel development in Western Christianity during the second half of the twentieth century. For is it not both interesting and odd that the corporate turning of attention towards the Far East of both Catholics and Protestants avid for spirituality grounded in ritualised physical discipline should have coincided with a thoroughgoing deritualisation of inherited forms of worship at home? This topic is a hot potato now, at any rate in Roman Catholic circles, where young people are keen to rediscover aspects of liturgy and ascetic practice abandoned in the wake of the Second Vatican Council – not, mostly, because the council required it, but because the council's reception to such an extent unfolded within the context of a cultural climate enthused by prospects of starting out afresh from clean slates through minimalist utilitarian means: the equivalence in ecclesiastical reform of Cripps's architecture.

Today's young seekers find themselves reprimanded by a

predominantly elderly establishment formed by the thrills and anxieties of that revolutionary time, which, to state the obvious, is chronologically further removed from them than the Treaty of Versailles was from youths waving banners on Parisian barricades in 1968, and in many ways quite as significant of a lost world. It is not my purpose to engage in polemics. What interests me, rather, is to explore an aspect of today's so-called liturgical 'conservatism' that I sense has been overlooked: namely, its physical and ascetic – if you like, its 'yogic' – aspect, which cannot be brushed aside, it seems to me, as an expression of a purportedly 'retrograde' or 'rigid' tendency, for it stands for the opposite: a yearning to be made *new* in Christ, and malleable. I will make my case by means of a brisk analysis of the ritual of the pre-conciliar Roman Missal, which can, over and above its sublime aspect, be read as a manual of sacred gymnastics.

The possibility of Mass taking place at all rests on two canons, 807–8, of the 1917 *Code of Canon Law*. Laying down parameters for licit celebration, they define that 'priests conscious of grave sin, no matter how contrite they believe themselves to be, shall not dare to celebrate Mass without prior sacramental confession'; next, that 'it is not licit for priests to celebrate without having observed a natural fast from midnight'. The celebrant is submitted to a discipline both moral and corporal. Soul and body are readied in advance for the Eucharistic sacrifice, which no one may presume to improvise. The ordained are to be configured to it, not it to them.

The requirement of fasting may have seemed innocuous enough to a cheerily rotund cathedral canon going to bed at 11 to rise at 6 and say Mass at 7, just downstairs, thereafter to tuck into sausages and eggs. But imagine being a priest in Nigeria, say, walking for hours in the forenoon sun to an outstation, carrying your portable altar on your back, without being able even to take a sip of water. Certain verses of the Psalms – 'My flesh faints for you' (63.1), 'My soul thirsts for you like a parched land' (143.6) – would seem overwhelmingly real, then. One would be conscious of the 'supersubstantial bread' as truly *nourishment*.

The double requirement of confession and fasting was incumbent not only on priests but on any Catholic going to Communion. In *The Burning Bush*, Sigrid Undset tells of the novel's hero Paul Selmer, a Catholic convert, attending a bridge night in stodgy gentlemanly company during World War I. The other players noticed that he did not refill his whisky-and-soda past midnight. Asked why, Paul said he would go to Mass in the morning and intended to receive the Sacrament. At this, the company was aghast. It is a trivial scene, in a way. At the same time it is a lofty one. It speaks of the deliberate integration of spiritual discipline into ordinary life; of an existence oriented, even in its social aspect, towards a transcendent goal.

No doubt some revision of the Church's rules was called for: the admission to break the fast with water, say, or medication. The erosion, though, went much further. The current rule is to fast for an hour before taking Communion, which more or less just rules out munching sandwiches *in the pews*, a practice from which most churchgoers would anyway refrain from considerations of courtesy.

A communicant under the old dispensation knew that the state of one's body is not indifferent to the state of one's soul. People these days must latch on to guru-dieticians for such insight, and are evidently hungry for it. Fasting is a fashionable lifestyle option now, but almost entirely divorced from the practice of faith.

The ritual also stipulates that a priest, before offering Mass, must recite Vigils and Lauds, then spend time in silent prayer. In today's secular context, this would be called a mindfulness exercise. He prepares the Missal and sacred vessels, then washes his hands, praying, 'Give strength to my hands, Lord, to wipe away every stain, that I may be apt to serve you in purity of mind and body.' The commitment implicit in his fasting is explicitly affirmed.

This is when the rite proper begins and all spontaneity ceases, much the way a woman or man attending a yoga class will, after warm-up, embark on a series of asanas minutely defined even in the subtle transitions from one to the next, requiring concentration and balance, enabling practitioners to be caught up in a movement that exceeds them. The priest is reminded that he is not the subject of the impending celebration; he is its vehicle. His task is to disappear into the words and gestures assigned to him, submitting, as a deliberate subject, to an objective reality.

The procedure of vesting recalls the last chapter of Ephesians which itemises the 'armour of God', associating specific parts of kit with distinct virtues (6.10–17). Taking the amice that covers his head like a hood before Mass, the priest asks the Lord to furnish a 'helmet of salvation' to ward off diabolical distraction. Putting on the alb, a linen garment covering his body, he prays that, 'washed in the Blood of the Lamb', he may live up to the grace won for him by obtaining a clean heart. Binding the cincture round his waist, he prays for continence and chaste strength. The maniple tied to his left arm is symbolically a handkerchief with which to wipe the tears he will not fail to weep if he invests himself in the Eucharistic mystery. The stole represents the primordial dignity of Adam issuing from God's creative hand: 'Restore to me, Lord', prays the priest, 'the stole of immortality I lost in my forefather's prevarication. I am unworthy to approach your great mystery! Grant me nonetheless to know eternal joy!' Finally, on top of all this comes the chasuble, symbolising Christ's sweet yoke, his light burden, held in place by strings wound tightly round the celebrant's body before being tied upon his heart in a knot. At this point he is like a soldier fit for battle, helmeted and cuirassed. The outward exercise of doffing ordinary garments and donning sacred ones prompts the interiorisation, day by day, of the Pauline injunction to shed the old man and put on the new.

The priest proceeds to the altar 'with eyes downcast, at a grave pace, his body held erect'. The postural specification regards the verticality specific to man, in which the Fathers saw a sign of dignity and a heavenward call. One does not approach the living God slouching. Yet the celebrant's attention is fixed on what lies ahead. He is not to look curiously around, but to focus on the task awaiting him, praying, 'I shall approach the altar of the Lord, the God who gives joy to my youth" (Psalm 43.4).

The liturgy begins at the altar steps, with the priest and acolyte performing a little set dialogue. It moves from a statement of purpose through a cry for God's help to a confession of sin. The priest confesses first. He receives the prayer for forgiveness from his minister, which is noteworthy. He cannot function at the altar unless, first, he is prayed for by a server, who traditionally has been a child. Thus he is exhorted, again, that he acts not in his own strength but in grace received – even as he openly confesses before, during, and after Mass his personal unworthiness.

To observe from a distance this preliminary rite, the ascent to the altar, then the unfolding of Mass is to witness, when the rubrics are carefully kept, a sacred choreography made up of steps to the right, a return to the centre, steps to the left, revolutions, genuflexions and bows, inclinations and benedictions, all within a continuous fluency of movement, quite as in a yogic session. The smallest gestures carry messages. A nod of the head shows a mention of the name of Jesus, his mother, or the saint of the day. The priest's bended knee, like Solomon's at the dedication of the temple, speaks of God's bright presence in his sanctuary. The priest is tactilely referenced to the altar, resting his hands there when they are not otherwise engaged, kissing it before turning round to address the congregation, visibly the altar's emissary. Even the configuration of his fingertips is kerygmatic.

What does this sort of practice do to a person performing it? All ritual can in theory become mindless performance, naturally. The secret is therefore to keep the mind engaged, the will mobilised, with *animus*, *anima*, and *spiritus* invested in the same unifying purpose: a corporate Godward movement in union with Christ, to render his saving sacrifice present and effective for the sustenance and sanctification of the Church. It requires presence of mind and determined self-surrender to keep this multitude of simultaneous prescriptions well. There is labour involved and notable mortification at first; but as the ritual gradually, with practice, becomes second nature, body and mind are freed, enabling a singular intensity of spiritual concentration. The intelligent daily repetition of such significant actions cannot but be formative. Outward actions impact for ill *or* good the conscious mind and sensitive spirit. Any yoga manual worth its salt will explain how this process works.

As for the assembly of the faithful drawn into the rite by means of an active participation properly theirs, what they behold is a person fully absorbed on their behalf by a noble, beautiful activity. Such a sight is always moving. Think of seeing Casals perform a cello suite by Bach or Margot Fonteyn dance the death of Giselle; think of watching an Olympic diver, a stone carver fixing a gaze of tenderness in marble, a delivery man unloading a palletful of Ming vases. The most venerable of human functions, the confection of Christ's Body and Blood in an act of rational worship, surely calls for no less a degree of deliberation and concentration.

It is this intuition, I believe, that stirs the hearts of many young women and men today. I cannot see that it is false. No, in a time weighed down by artificiality, leaden rhetoric, dud personality cults, and frantic 'innovations' of terrifying banality in stagecraft, political campaigning, *and* liturgical practice, a quest for objective, oblative expression in sacred functions appears to me sound and forward-looking.

I hazard a further proposition, aware of the risk attached. The Catholic Church lives with a modern legacy of clerical abuse that constitutes an open gash in the ecclesiastical Body. Abuse is an age-old phenomenon present in every period, each cultural environment; in our day, other churches and institutions, too, are afflicted by it. At one level it pertains to a timeless *mysterium iniquitatis* and to man's capacity for wickedness. There seems to be no doubt, though, that the incidence of priestly abuse in the Roman Catholic Church rose sharply from the early 1960s, coinciding with the relinquishing of physical, ritual, and moral discipline in life and worship.

Clearly, many priests had found the old liturgical form – the Mass with its inflexible rubrics, sixteen genuflexions, and fifty-two signs of the cross – suffocating. Many were hungry for spontaneous expression. What followed was the often tedious, sometimes destructive emergence of the priest as *personality*. Whether or not endowed with much charisma, whether or not a learned theologian or able preacher, he found himself in the centre as service-provider and visual focus of attention, with substantial executive freedom to mould rites to his form and whim, promoting or discarding at will others' partaking. It is documented that physical abuse is almost always prepared and preceded by spiritual manipulation sprung from claims to personal authority or even fancied omnipotence based on some delusional, semi-mystical idea amounting to the claim: 'I am special; I am in charge; I do as I please'.

All of us are susceptible to such megalomaniac illusion. The more closely we are associated with a sacred office, the more potentially lethal and luciferian this tendency becomes, inflating our perception of self. There may have been wisdom in a regimen that ascetically reined in the presumption of sacred ministers, requiring them daily to regulate their appetites, to restate multiple times their vocational purpose, to enact an intricate ritual calling for an *ex officio* obliteration of self, thereby to grow in the grace of discipleship and to be effective, Christophorus channels of grace, not deluding themselves for a moment that they are somehow grace's *source*.

I am not saying that the answer to all today's ecclesiastical traumas is found in a return to old usages. Complex issues do not have such easy remedies, alas. What I am saying is this: It seems short-sighted to brush aside the hunger of many young Christians for ritual, ascesis, symbols, and formality by branding it as imbecile nostalgia, with the supreme indictment of it being anti-modern, anti-inclusive, or, in a Catholic context, anti-conciliar. The watchword of Vatican II was: 'Return to the sources!' To drink deeply from the sources is precisely what the young want. Why not help them? Why not enable them to find within their own tradition a patrimony rightfully theirs, time-tested practices apt to help them grow in Christ instead of leaving them to the vaguely ethereal hunches of Steve Jobs?

The great Christian problem today is the problem of the human person and of the human body. We need a Christocentric conversion in mind and manners to make sense of our significant being, to account for our origin and end, our longings and frustrations, our wounds and our capacity for healing. To engage and counter a secular insinuation that 'I' – whatever 'I' might be – am a stranger in my body and that my body is potentially inimical to 'me', we need a revival of William of Saint-Thierry's reasoned conviction that my body *is* me, that its call is noble, even beatific, inseparable from the potential of my intellective and spiritual faculties. We may find then that our endeavour to operate a personal union of *animus*, *anima*, and *spiritus* does not necessarily need to take a detour via yoga. The Christian West could do with recovering a love for and a confidence in its own tradition, much the way the Cistercians did in the twelfth century, inaugurating a period of manifold flourishing.

Why cross the river in order to draw water? The Church has vast experience when it comes to the embodied application of Christian faith in God's Incarnation, which elevates our nature indescribably. Christians have sought to join the body to the spirit's pursuits in various ways. My superficial perusal of the ritual pointed towards a particular treasure. There are others. A reevaluation of Christian fasting is overdue. Much can be learnt from the ascesis of monastics, at once idealists and realists. The practice of prostrations in prayer is worthy of recovery; it is a feature not just of Byzantine piety but also, in the West, of Cistercian, Carthusian, and Mendicant devotion. Processions and pilgrimages, prominent in our tradition, provide privileged means of exercising the body in prayer. And of course, there is the prayer of the heart, whose blatantly physical aspect can appear disconcerting.

The best modern disquisition known to me on this subject happens to be of Western origin. It is a treatise written by Dom André Poisson, prior of La Grande Chartreuse, so superior general of the Carthusian Order, from 1967–97, the decades during which so many Western Christians turned towards the Far East in search of body-spirit unity. The treatise, dated 'Christmas 1983', is redolent with the grace of the Word's Incarnation, ever the foundation of Christian anthropology.

Dom Poisson insists that the 'prayer of the heart' cannot be reduced to an abstraction, as if the 'heart', in this instance, were purely symbolic. 'Every movement of the heart', he says, 'that contributes to our relation with the Father is linked to our sensible, material being. From experience, perhaps at some cost to our health, we know that truly profound emotions attain our physical heart.' He stresses that 'we cannot enter the prayer of the heart unless we accept to live deliberately and determinedly at the level of our body'. Why do we find this so hard to take on board within our normal setting, looking instead for exotic practices and new idioms?

Possibly because we tend to live and think as implicit dualists, conceiving of our bodies as repositories of appetites, pains, pleasures, and intimate excretions with no bearing on what we think of as our 'higher' self, as unwieldy frames of which we are often embarrassed, so that we rule out their involvement in the realisation of our theological finality. Do we in fact own our body as a place of encounter with God, not just in the *eschaton* but now? Do we believe in the body's fitness for resurrection?

Dom Poisson, truly a monk and therefore a person steeped in liturgy, develops his perspective within a Eucharistic ecclesiology: 'Even as it is impossible to approach life in community as if our brothers were disincarnate beings of pure spirit, to be reached somehow beyond their physical wrapping, it would be a denial of the reality of God's love to turn the physical, material, palpable presence of the Son-with-us into an abstraction.' Saint Antony the Great said, 'With our neighbour is life and death', an insight Saint Silouan of Athos distilled into 'My brother is my life'. That affirmation is at once experiential and conceptual, enabled by a mystery of Communion effected through material realities that *are* the Son of God. 'Similarly', writes Dom Poisson – and there is considerable daring in that only apparently casual adverb –

> Similarly, our own body, with its heaviness, limits, and constraints, is the reality of what we are. It is my body that touches that other reality of which Jesus said: 'This is my Body.' . . . I cannot possibly pray without praying in my body. When I turn towards God, I cannot abstract my incarnate reality. It is not just a question of religious discipline if certain gestures are prescribed, if certain material conditions direct me, when I turn to God. These are pointers to the one and only truth: God loves me the way he made me. Why should I want to be more spiritual than he?

The question is rhetorical. It nonetheless challenges a number of ecclesiastical projects, strategies, reforms, and synodal ventures of the past six or seven decades, during which the Church, right smack in the middle of the sexual revolution, has often tended, weirdly, to leave the body behind, preferring concepts to *praxis*. Impatience with this state of affairs seems to me a sign of Christian health. Before us on the horizon, as I write, is the seventeenth centenary of the Council of Nicaea at which the Church of East and West proclaimed with one voice the reality of the Word's Incarnation. It would seem a fitting opportunity to reaffirm the grace bestowed thereby upon our flesh, and the prospect of worshipful dignity such grace enables.

4

The Monastery as *SCHOLA DEI*

A paper given at a conference organised at Princeton by the Aquinas Institute's Program in Catholic Thought on 25–26 October 2024 under the title 'Beyond the Impasse: Theological Perspectives on DEI'.

In his prologue to the Holy Rule, written up in the late fifth century and destined to become, unbeknownst to its author, a key source for the development of European civilisation, Saint Benedict calls the monastery, a term still possessed in his day of beguiling potential, *dominici schola servitii* (Prologue 45). This phrase is usually rendered 'a school of the Lord's service', suggesting the image of a bearded old monk at his board taking novices through the ABCs of ascetic living. The association is not entirely false, but inadequate. A *schola* in Latin antiquity was not an institution much like what we think of now as a 'school'. Something of the ancient sense was kept in Italian. Visitors to Venice will know the Scuola of San Rocco or of San Teodoro. The Venetian *scuole* were lay associations that sometimes resembled trade unions or foreigners' clubs, microsocieties within the framework of the republic providing for their members welfare, a social network, and professional support. Think, too, of Renaissance painters whose pupils produced work under their instruction, canvases curators now attribute to 'the School of Michelangelo' or 'the School of Titian'. These associations help us to understand the Benedictine project on its own terms.

The *schola* Benedict speaks of is a place in which knowledge is imparted, yes; even more essentially it is a place of enterprise in which something new is created. That something is a novel model of community binding men freely together by means of a covenant of life and a clear purpose. For take note: Benedict stresses that his Rule is for 'the strong race of coenobites' (1.13) — that is, of people resolved to foster togetherness, be it at some cost to their preference or comfort. The word 'coenobite' derives from Greek. It is made up of two elements: the adjective κοινός, meaning 'common' in the sense of 'shared', and βίος, which means 'life', as in 'biology', discourse about living things. In the first chapter of the Rule, Benedict contrasts coenobites with three other types of monks. Let us consider them briefly.

First, there are hermits going 'from the battle line in the ranks of their brothers to the single combat of the desert' (1.2–5). Benedict's choice of martial imagery is revealing. It is foolish to go out into the desert, a dangerous place, without having first rubbed shoulders with others in a school of discipline. The Christian hermit is no mere opter-out. His combat is motivated by universal charity. Separated from everything, in Evagrius's phrase, he is united with all and makes his oblation on behalf of all. For this end to be realised, his love must be awakened, purified, and tested in human company. The Christian *ethos* is wary of abstractions. It calls for authentication in terms of real philanthropy. This requirement sets it apart from ideologies whose end may be sublime, but whose means for arriving at it are botched, like that of the Rusanovs in Solzhenitsyn's

Cancer Ward, who loved 'the People, their great People, served the People and were ready to give their lives for the People', but who 'found themselves less and less able to tolerate actual human beings, those obstinate creatures who were always resistant, refusing to do what they were told to and, besides, demanding something for themselves.' Cenobitic discipline relieves a man of illusions about mankind and about himself. It teaches him to face humanity in its complexity, with its inward and outward contradictions, its noises and smells, *and* with its capacity for greatness. Instead of dreaming up a notional 'People', he learns, through battle, to love people as they are.

Next, there are the sarabites (1.6–9). No one really knows what this name means, but it stands for an aberration. Benedict calls the sarabites detestable, 'monachorum taeterrimum genus', a strong word to flow from the quill of one so measured in speech. When we read how he describes them, we are embarrassed. For the sarabites are uncannily like us. Their character is 'soft as lead'. Though religious in appearance, they display by their actions that they are 'still loyal to the world'. They huddle in small groups of like-minded folk, so as not to be disturbed in their notions. 'Their law is what they like to do, whatever strikes their fancy. Anything they believe in and choose, they call holy; anything they dislike, they consider forbidden.' The paradigm may allow us to recognise groups we meet in our daily lives, who 'pen themselves up in their own sheepfold'. The temptation is real. Vigilance is called for.

Finally, Benedict presents the gyrovagues (1.10–11). A *gyrovagus* is literally someone who goes round and round. He despises linearity and is therefore unlikely to make any kind of meaningful progress. A gyrovague is at one and the same time a lone wolf, a window-shopper, and a sponge. Gyrovagues, we read in the Rule, are 'always on the move, never settle down, slaves to their self-will and gross appetites'. They strategically knock on lots of different doors, ever guests in others' houses, never staying long but always filling their tummies, unable to set up a lasting home for themselves. Here, too, we recognise a type of person abroad in our time, where circular movement damned to non-arrival unfolds not only in material space or within the intricate confines of a person's mind, but in the vast, waterless wastes of the internet. In every way, says Benedict, gyrovagues 'are worse than sarabites'. They bar themselves from ever reaching happiness. Enough said.

This brief overview, a Benedictine sociology of types, gives us an idea of key lessons imparted in the *dominici schola servitii*. One learns, there, the self-knowledge vital for any societal enterprise; one learns perseverance and humility by staying over time in committed fellowship with others; one learns to temper one's appetites and to still one's anger; one learns to serve charitably; and one learns patience, that Christian hallmark, potentially of great moral stature.

In Christian terms, it is legitimate, I think, to relabel this school a *SCHOLA DEI*. The genitive construction sustains, in Latin, two senses. It can refer to the object of learning: in this instance, life according to God's call, revealed in Christ. And it can refer to the teaching subject, God himself, working through human instruments and circumstances. It is not, then, by mere facetiousness that I have titled my essay by adopting the acronym of the conference theme. In fact, the values of diversity, equity, and inclusion (DEI) do condition Benedict's enterprise. For a millennium and a half, his rule has proved a paradigm for contented human coexistence.

Might it have something to tell us regarding challenges we face now, AD 2025? I think so. So I shall consider the elements of DEI from a Benedictine perspective. It makes sense to set out from 'inclusion'. Therefore, I shall work through the letters backwards.

INCLUSION

The Benedictine monastery is in principle, and in practice, a place where everyone is welcome in. It is hospitable. A monastery 'is never without guests', says Benedict, for whom that affirmation is simply a description of how things are and should be. This tight-knit, regular society has a porous boundary. Part of its ascesis is readiness to be disturbed by people turning up needing time, attention, and compassionate help. For the guests we are talking about are not just devout retreatants calling in for a few days of restful silence. The Rule speaks of 'poor people and pilgrims', the latter term meaning 'people arrived from abroad', on a journey God knows where, perhaps just in search of livelihood. In these, we are told, Christ is most particularly received. They are to be welcomed with 'great care and concern', graciously (53.15–16).

How this is to be done is shown in two specific counsels. We find the first in the chapter on the porter, who is a living conduit between the resident community and the world round about. He is the monastery's public face and – at the same time, before the community – ambassador of those who turn up at the door. He should be a *senex sapiens*, 'a wise elder'. This title has a venerable aspect suggesting maturity of insight and charity. It carries, too, a note of humorous realism. The porter's age, says Benedict, 'will keep him from roaming about'. He will be apt to sit quietly in his lodge – doing what? Primarily, his business is to wait. He is there to ensure that no one who knocks will be without a friendly welcome and a good word: 'As soon as anyone knocks, or a poor man calls out, he replies, "Thanks be to God" or "Your blessing, please"; then, with all the gentleness that comes from the fear of God, he provides a prompt answer with the warmth of love.'

Gentleness, promptness, and the warmth of love are to be extended to *everyone*. The porter is mobilised on these terms before he has even seen with whom he is dealing. Greeting the knock with the cry, 'Deo gratias', he employs the formula used at Mass to acclaim the Word of God. In the needs of a stranger, he welcomes, and seeks to understand, a divine call. He may also shout, 'Benedic' — that is, 'Your blessing, please!' — conscious that each human being, however destitute, is the bearer of some unique goodness to be received as a gift from God. From the start, the encounter between insider and outsider is marked by reciprocity and, thus, by respect (66.1–4).

A guest is by definition a bird of passage. What of those come to settle? Here there is a noteworthy contrast. Where the guest is received with exquisite kindness, the aspiring novice is tested. The Rule commands, 'Do not grant newcomers an easy entry'. Then it goes on to prescribe treatment that may seem to us a little savage: 'If someone comes and keeps knocking at the door, and if at the end of four or five days he has shown himself patient in bearing his harsh treatment and difficulty of entry, and has persisted in his request, then he should be allowed to enter and stay in the guesthouse for a few days.' During his time of waiting he will either have been camping outside or have kept coming and going. The keyword in this passage is 'patient'. The procedure Benedict outlines intends to help the candidate examine himself and his motives. Is this what he really wants? Does he have the staying power for it? These are key questions to ask of anyone seeking to become part of a stable human community.

One who perseveres through testing is to be let into the novitiate, there to be looked after by 'a senior chosen for his skill in winning souls'. This seasoned monk has one principal task: to verify 'whether the novice truly seeks God'. This is really Benedict's sole criterion of vocation discernment. It has an eminently practical side. The novice must work out whether what he seeks is what the community proposes, whether his personal goals are aligned to those among whom he wishes to pitch his tent. Fruitful, peaceful coexistence presupposes unity of vision. A newcomer is therefore, for his own good, taught a lesson of realism. Outwardly, this involves an account of 'the hardships and difficulties that will lead him to God'. He is to be made acquainted with the monastic rule. During his novitiate, it is read through to him thrice in entirety. He is told, 'This is the law under which you are choosing to serve. If you can keep it, come in. If not, feel free to leave.' The stress on freedom is capital. It flows from the groundswell of the Christian condition. But this imperative of freedom is spelled out in view of oblation, not of narcissistic self-realisation. Human beings exist, from a Christian point of view, for self-giving, for the binding in truth of their affection: sarabitical withdrawal or vague gyrovagueries cannot satisfy the yearning of their soul. To grow up, a man needs to purify and freely direct his will (58.1–29).

The novice must for this reason come to know himself. What animates me? What makes me afraid? What do I desire? Where am I shackled? Where do I need restraint? The grand seventh chapter of the rule, 'On Humility', is a manual of such enquiry, to be conducted before God in a logic of trustful obedience to a spiritual father, for 'inclusion' here entails entrusting oneself to a personal communion, not just carving out a space for oneself. A monastic pedagogy of self-knowledge differs from manoeuvring within the number-coded web of the enneagram. It is performed to enable not merely self-acceptance, which is but a propaedeutic stage, but self-transcendence. That is why fraternal relations are always the acid test of genuine progress. The Rule's injunctions are clear: 'Help the troubled and console the sorrowing. . . . Do not act in anger or bear a grudge. Rid your heart of all deceit. Never give a hollow greeting of peace or turn away when someone needs your love' (4.18, 22–26). When such responses, by the interplay of determination and grace, slowly become second nature, the monk ceases to be a borrowed ace within an unsteady house of cards. He becomes instead a constituent part of a living body, transplanted into what Benedict calls the *corpus monasterii* as a living member. And is it not indeed the case that genuine 'inclusion' is a matter of incorporation, requiring vital, subtle transfusions from the receiving organism *and* back, for the thriving of the whole?

EQUITY

The word 'equity' is polyvalent. It is commonly used in the discourse of finance to indicate stocks or shares shifted, bought, and sold to make an income. On hearing 'equity' spoken, we are conditioned to ask, 'What's in it for me?' In the context of DEI, the ethical sense of 'equity' is to the fore, naturally. Still, the economic, we might say capitalist, resonance should be born in mind. This concords with a definition of 'equity' I found in a 2022 article published by McKinsey & Company: 'Equity refers to fair treatment for all people, so that the norms, practices, and policies in place ensure identity is not predictive of opportunities or workplace outcomes. Equity differs from equality in a subtle but important way. While equality assumes that all people should be treated the same, equity takes into consideration a person's unique circumstances, adjusting treatment accordingly so that the end result is equal.'

But equal on what terms? There is scope here for application corresponding to that of Orwell's pigs, who in an equity manifesto declared all animals equal, but some just a bit 'more equal' than others. The McKinsey definition of equity ties up with notions of entitlement. Its point of departure is 'identity'. No one's identity should *a priori* be 'predictive of opportunities or . . . outcomes'. At this point tension arises. 'Opportunities' belong in the realm of objective reference, whereas 'identity', in the world in which we live, is largely subjective. As such, it is holy ground, for no one must challenge another's perceived or projected sense of self. This is not the time to go into this problem. My point is this, simply: In today's secular speech, 'identity' spells acquisition, the shares *I* invest in corporate enterprise, expecting these to correspond without any prejudice to my expected margin of gain.

If we turn back to the Rule, we find ourselves engaging with other categories. As legislator, Benedict is concerned with justice. To apply this virtue in practice, he conceives of 'equity' in terms of 'equilibration'. Benedict is less seduced by 'equality' than modern theoreticians. Experience has taught him that it can be an oppressive term, insensitive to the requirements of circumstance. Take his chapters on the right measure of food and drink. He provides a norm, a pretty ample one (a pound of bread and a half-bottle of wine per monk per day), only to stress that 'everyone has his own gift from God, one this and another that', so that it is 'with some unease that we specify the amount of food and drink for others': what is right for one is too little, or too much, for his neighbour. When work is heavy and the weather hot, the abbot may exercise discretion, making sure that each receives what he needs, taking care only 'that over-indulgence is avoided, lest a monk experience a surfeit' (39.4; 40.1–3).

This pragmatic passage expresses the tenor of the Rule in matters of equity by positing as a marker of identity first giftedness, then weakness. The incorporation of a member enriches the body; at the same time, the frailties of each affect the whole. The receiving of a gift calls for gratitude; confrontation with necessity, for mercy. These complementary responses build up monastic society and point, in concert, towards a principle that defines it: Benedict stresses that the monks must 'honour' one another (4.8; 53.2). They are to be respectful, that is, of each other's irreducible alterity, conscious of the mystery each embodies, discerning in each other a reflection of the image in which all are uniquely made. Gratitude, mercy, honour: If we are concerned about equity, these are the qualities by which it is recognised.

In terms of 'opportunities' and 'outcomes', Benedict's focus is not on private gain. Indeed, those who enter Benedictine society forego prospects of gain for ever, offering up their persons in their intellectual, moral, and physical aspects (33.4). Petty ambition, like that of the artisan seeking distinction from his wares (57.2–3), and secret hoarding, stashes under the mattress, compromise the monk's supernatural and civic engagement (55.16). Sliding down such slopes, he dishonours himself. The finality of his life is transcendent: 'That in all things God should be glorified' (57.9). This aim is pursued in a life of worship; in enterprise striving to instantiate work the way Adam first knew it, as beatitude (for it was sin that made work drudgery); in shared happiness, the yearning for 'good days' being a vocational requirement for monks (Prol. 15); and in gradual delivery from that cruelest of tyrants, which Benedict calls *voluntas propria*, 'self-will', the ensemble of my intimate addictions and obsessions, *idées fixes*, and reasons for self-pity, patterns of thought and behaviour that shut me up in myself and off from others. Such mortification of self-will is no obliteration of personhood. Benedict would utterly recoil from the idea of turning a man into an automaton. That which must go is my tendency to see myself as the sun in a universe of extinguished stars, a temptation that, for all its patent absurdity, is surprisingly hard to eliminate.

Since freedom from attachment is part of the goal a monk pursues, personal forfeiture of 'equity' in the McKinseyan sense can be laudable. Benedict devotes a chapter to the question 'Whether all should receive necessaries equally?', inviting a realist perspective infused with charity, concerned with legitimate needs. Then he lays down: 'Let whoever needs less thank God and not be distressed; let whoever needs more feel humble because of his weakness, not self-important because of kindness shown him' (34.3–4). Both need and the absence of need become opportunities to foster a *eucharistic* mindset investing a person, and potentially a community of persons, with graciousness, an endowment mere calculation is powerless to bestow.

As far as deliberations are concerned, Benedict is wholly equitable. While the monastery is governed hierarchically, with the abbot seen to 'hold the place of Christ', it is not totalitarian. The abbot is above all bound to the Rule and recalled to his fallibility. In all matters of consequence, he is to take counsel (2.2, 40; 3.1, 12).

The brothers have a right and duty to express their opinions. *All* are to be heard, even the newly arrived, 'since the Lord often reveals what is better to the younger' (3.3). For a fifth-century Roman text, this statement is extraordinary, redolent with the radicalism that ever complements monks' conservative instincts. Secular or inherited status shall play no role at all: 'a man born free is not to be given higher rank than a slave who becomes a monk' (2.18). Were Benedict writing now, he might have added that felt inherited disadvantage should no more be a reason for preferential treatment. He urges us constantly to see beyond conditioning: to perceive ourselves afresh, at once unafraid of our poverty and determined to rise to our human and Christian dignity, thereby apt to see others, too, with purity of vision, loving inquisitiveness, and hope.

DIVERSITY

Anyone seeing a monastic community processing into church for vespers will be struck by its uniformity. The monks wear the same clothes, follow the same pace, replicate the same gestures, and, ideally, sing in tune. Anyone who knows a community personally, meanwhile, will be struck by its often frankly improbable variety. There is something about monastic life that, when it works, *liberates* character. For years I have reflected on something Ingmar Bergman once said about his films: The elaboration of complex material calls for rigour of form. Monastic life provides for those called to it a formative structure enabling personhood to flourish.

To consider Benedictine intellectual and artistic output over a millennium and a half is to behold great diversity of sensibilities and temperaments. Further, monks and nuns have inculturated themselves into every continent, able to integrate ethnic, linguistic, and cultural diversity while maintaining a brand instantly recognisable as Benedictine. There is something Terentian about monasticism. The dictum 'Nothing human is foreign to me' is reflected in its annals. Monastic hagiography puts in relief every human variant. Diversity is from the outset a monastic trait. This point does not need to be laboured. I would like instead to focus on safeguards envisaged to keep diversity within helpful bounds, preventing it from undermining the community's oneness and from descending into mere singularity.

'Singularity' in monastic parlance is a pernicious expression of self-will as I defined it above. By singular comportment, I deviate from the common rhythm and rule. I yield to a childish desire for attention, wanting to be seen. I wish others to recognise my talents or wounds, to admire or feel sorry for me. Making of *me* the focus of existence, I seek affirmation and comfort. I ask for dispensations from the common life, which has come to seem to me heavy and dull; or I simply isolate myself, pleading personal need or some irreducible vulnerability. I feel overlooked, underappreciated, and unwanted. Before long, I shall be indulging in a vice Benedict censures strictly, knowing what havoc it can wreak: I shall start to murmur.

Murmuring is a form of passive aggression amply instantiated in the Bible. A murmur is different from a lament. To lament is to call out in distress, to articulate pain, to let anguish out in a cry for help, be it hyperbolically or even irrationally. That is an honest business: the puss must out. Murmuring, by contrast, is self-indulgent, calculating, and vindictive. The murmurer shirks responsibility, blaming others for real or felt misfortune. He or she instrumentalises hardship or perceived slights to spread discontent and undermine authority, pointing the finger at others, the way

Israel did in the desert, pining for the cucumbers of Egypt, bored with the exodus they had freely chosen to share, hissing at Moses: '*You* have brought us out into this wilderness' (Exodus 16.3).

In the setting of monasticism, Benedict flags the risk of murmuring in these situations, readily transferrable to other walks of life: when a monk is asked, for the common good, to undertake a task he feels is beneath him; when he feels someone else receives preferential treatment he would want for himself; when he thinks too much is asked of him; when he does not get his ration of wine (5.14ff.; 34.6; 35.13; 40.8f.). By murmuring, he effectively retracts the oblation of self that is the covenantal glue of his vocation, the foundation for the 'good days' he once sought ecstatically, *outside* himself, looking up and around. Descending from the crystalline altitudes of God, he retreats into the moist armpit of self. When appeals to self-centred 'difference' divert a man from society and spawn tyrannical claims to privilege, they engage passions of the soul that militate against spiritual freedom. Caught in these, I have eyes only for myself. My own murmuring soon becomes the only tune to which my ears are attuned.

It is tiresome to live with murmurers. Yet murmuring does its worst harm to those indulging in it. It locks them out of the real world and into a world of fantasy. That is why Benedict counters it with his strongest sanction: excommunication. An inveterate murmurer is to be warned twice in private. The point is to try to make him see the harm he does himself and others. If that does not work, he is to be rebuked before all. 'If even then he does not reform, let him be excommunicated' (23.1–5). Excommunication is enacted in degrees, according to the seriousness of the fault. First, it entails exclusion from the common table; next, from both table and oratory, causing the brother to eat and pray alone. In serious cases, a monk is excluded from all human contact: 'No brother should associate or converse with him at all'; to do so would itself provoke a sanction (25–26). This punishment has an educative purpose. It is meant to make the monk understand: By acting like this, you break down fellowship. Excommunication should be an eye-opener, inducing the wanderer to come back into the fold. It is a means by which the abbot exercises his ministry as shepherd, striving by all means to bring the stray sheep back, if need be by picking it up and carrying it on his shoulders (27.9).

Benedict would not be Benedict, though, were he to leave it at that. The chapters on excommunication are followed by one 'On the abbot's care for the excommunicated'. It is a remarkable text. Benedict acknowledges that the abbot has sometimes to be inflexible, fixing and guarding limits. At the same time, he must seek to reach, comfort, and guide the one shut out. Unable to do so himself, as the Rule's guardian, he sends ambassadors, wise monks dispatched 'under the cloak of secrecy' to support the wavering brother 'lest he be overwhelmed by excessive sorrow'. He delicately qualifies the sternness of a righteous judge with 'the skill of a wise physician' (27.1–4). His task is to unite his diverse companions in harmony, to let the genius of each enrich and embellish the whole. Diversity is problematic only when it generates centrifugal tendencies, fragmenting instead of complementing, fostering secession, not a desire to belong. To maintain the delicate balance of plurality in oneness, a corporate purpose is needed that exceeds the mere sum of constituent parts. The body must be called to rise towards transfiguration, engaged all the while in a mission to ensure the health of each member in view of integral flourishing. Where a toe is fixated on being just a toe, absorbed perhaps by the discomfort of an ingrown nail, it deprives itself of the joy of bearing up a physiognomy in forward movement, proceeding coordinatedly along a royal road bound for home.

CONCLUSION

DEI stands for values germane to a Benedictine model of society. Each, though, has a destructive flip side. 'Inclusion' is good for building up communion; as a slogan of entitlement, it is noxious. 'Equity' is splendid as a marker of societal equilibration; hijacked in view of private gain, it can become a tool of manipulation. 'Diversity' is lovely showing forth the complementarity of gifts; enclosing people in self-affirming apartness, its fruits are bitter, causing indigestion in the body politic. To be beneficial, the just exercise of these qualities has to be learnt. It is not anodyne, then, to speak of a *SCHOLA DEI*. We need purposeful formation to be equitable, inclusive, and diverse in truth, even as we must be taught how to be, and help others be, truly free.

A rhetorical, caricatural exploitation of these terms has led to an impasse. The word is well chosen: it indicates a point from which normally no forward movement is possible, only retraction. Positions are locked, passions run high. There are shouting matches. To respond to rhetoric and caricature cynically by these same means is unproductive though, and ridiculous, really. It is worth reflecting that pedalling back is the sole way out of an impasse only if the obstacle cannot be overcome. But what if it can? We read in a Psalm of David, 'By my God I can leap over a wall' (Psalm 18.29). The principle is timeless. Discouragement is for the faint-hearted.

There is too much good at stake, too much goodwill existing in the midst of some evident craziness, for us to watch placidly while the terms of DEI are undermined, then shoved into the compost. And is there not a growing heap? For a while, DEI has been politically and commercially exploited. Why not use it if it sells? Customers show signs of having had enough though. The recent foreswearing of DEI by, for example, Toyota likely indicates a growing trend. It is in the nature of slogans, especially acronyms, to last but a season. Seasons in trade and fashion are short.

The vacuity of much discourse on this theme results from the absence of a viable metanarrative, of an overarching anthropological vision. To make sense, the terms of DEI must be defined. Inclusion into what? Equity by what just standard? Diversity according to what norm? These are questions our pragmatic times are ill-equipped to handle and from which public figures shirk. For to pass from the register of 'How?' to that of 'Why?' presupposes commitment to a worldview, and even to envisage such a thing is considered by many to be manifestly anti-DEI. This is the irony, in some sense the tragedy, we must address. The task presents a challenge for society as a whole but for Christians especially, held as they are to a vision of a new heaven and a new earth (see Revelation 21.1), the prospect of which is not reserved for the *eschaton*. The Church is to be, here and now, 'a lasting, sure seed of unity, hope and salvation for the whole human race'. That's an instruction! Hope seems to me here the crucial term. Many of our time's ideological excesses are customised attempts to recreate it, for it is long gone from politics. We miss it, be it subliminally. Yet hope cannot be decreed as strategy. It must be born.

For centuries, the civilisational mission of the Church has found expression in charitable enterprise, in liturgy and the arts, in intellectual endeavour. It has expressed itself, too, no less durably, in the repristination of vocabulary, enabling Christians to rescue from mythicised mists precious notions needed to speak afresh a common, desirable human purpose. Controversies provoked by DEI show the want of such purpose in a society whose fabric is unravelling in all directions at once, from which whole spools of thread are brusquely extracted, in which patterns of nobility or beauty no longer appear to the naked eye. Saint Benedict lived in a world that, in this respect, resembled ours, a twilight world. His response was, in the words of a Psalm, to 'awake the dawn' (Psalm 108.2). He reminded man, for whom it is not good to be alone (see Genesis 2.18), experientially of what it is to be fully and happily human in order, next, to frame that proposition by way of a sharable ideal. The method has worked in the past, drawing forth from different sensibilities a most gracious quality: *unanimitas*, a oneness of soul that makes heavy things light. Who knows? It might work again. For truly, what is needed now is more than merely a wearily doctored political agenda. What is needed is a new sense of the very notion of a *polis*. What is needed is a rebirth of man. Needed is a credibly embodied, corporate witness to true humanity.

5

Repairing the Wound

Je suis une morte vivante pour la vie. À 66 ans, je suis tellement vide que j'ai du mal à trouver les mots pour me révolter contre toi.

I am, for life, a dead woman alive. At the age of sixty-six, I am so utterly empty that I find it hard to find words to rise up in revolt against you.

—Testimony of Catherine, cited in the *Sauvé Report*

An aspect of the Mass that strikes me more and more as the years pass is the stress placed, in the final prayers that precede Holy Communion, on healing. At the elevation, the priest holds up the Body of Christ, inviting the assembly to recognise in it the Lamb of God 'who takes away the sins of the world'. The assembly responds, 'Lord I am not worthy that you should enter under my roof, but only say the word and my soul shall be healed.' This acclamation makes explicit a sentiment the priest has just voiced quietly in two prayers assigned to him alone. One senses that celebrants do not always give them the attention they deserve.

In the first prayer, the priests asks for mercy and protection for himself: 'Free me by this, your most holy Body and Blood, from all my sins and from every evil; keep me always faithful to your commandments and never let me be parted from you.' It is the prayer of Adam redeemed, resolved never again to retreat into the bushes. It is a prayer that says, 'Heal me, God, from the allurement of the dark!' The second prayer asks that we may not stand condemned by the Holy Sacrifice – condemned, that is, by the fact that our lives do not correspond to what the Sacrament signifies. The priest prays that it may be for him, through God's mercy, 'protection in mind and body and a healing remedy'. The phrasing of the Latin text has a slightly different emphasis: 'Prosit mini . . . ad medelam percipiendam'. That is to say, 'May it benefit me in such a way that I'll be apt to receive healing'. Embedded within this phrase is the Lord's challenge to the paralytic by the pool: to obtain healing, we must want it and arrange our priorities accordingly.

These prayers of the Missal reflect a key insight of the primitive Church. One of the earliest extra-biblical definitions we have of the Lord's Supper is a reference in Ignatius of Antioch's *Letter to the Ephesians*. Ignatius calls the Eucharist φάρμακον ἀθανασίας, 'the medicine of immortality'. Death is the ailment for which the Eucharist is principally a remedy. And death, we know, is 'the wages of sin' (Romans 6:23). We would commit a mistake if we somehow tried to separate the Eucharist from the effective unfolding of our redemption. The healing it provides is not of the order of hot towels, essential oils, and honeyed infusions.

The Eucharist must not be cosified. Nor must it be reduced to the inoffensive status of a devotion. It is, and is intended to be, a stumbling block, rooted in the mystery of Christ as such. Ignatius refers to it as φάρμακον just after promising to send the Ephesians a further tract 'concerning the dispensation of the new man Jesus Christ, . . . dealing with his faith and his love, his suffering and his resurrection'. Any perspective on the Eucharist narrower than this is inadequate. We must aspire to understand the Sacrament in terms of the whole mystery of Christ, as an agent of death's destruction.

The healing efficacy of the Eucharist resides in the way it incorporates us into the mystery of Christ. Eucharistic healing is different from Hippocratic healing. The latter is geared towards the preservation of life. The former makes us capable of laying down our lives. Again Ignatius of Antioch provides food for thought. An exceptional statement from his *Letter to the Romans* should be allowed to complement his words about the 'medicine of immortality'. It was written when the prospect of martyrdom had drawn close. He asks the Christians in Rome not to prevent him, by misguided good will, from offering his life: 'Forgive me, brethren; hinder me not from living. Do not wish me to die. Do not give to the world one who desires to belong to God, nor deceive him with material things. Let me receive the pure light; arrived at that point, I shall become a man [ἐκεῖ παραγενόμενος ἄνθρωπος ἔσομαι]'. Ignatius, the faithful bishop, who had administered the Sacrament with fortitude, is emphatic: His wounded humanity will be fully restored only when he, in communion with his Master, makes of his life a holocaust. This is a noble example for us all, sprung from a high ideal.

Alas, this ideal has all too often been trampled in the dirt by men who were supposed to embody it and to be transformed by it.

During the past week or two, I have been reading the *Sauvé Report* on abuse in the French church during the past seventy years. It is an exceptionally difficult read. The abuse scandal is a matter we all would prefer not to think about. The relentless, apparently unending unravelling of awfulness can seem more than we can bear. But we have to face it. Only the truth sets us free.

The *Sauvé Report* includes lengthy extracts from the testimonies of survivors. I remain haunted by the following statement from Martin, who as a very young man was sexually abused by a priest: 'The bastard crushed any real feelings of love and compassion in me. I've been left with a handicap in love, unable either to give or receive it. I've had to just pretend. But what is a life without love?' Dear God, what a terrible, terrible indictment! And this harm was wrought by a man who should have been a minister of the φάρμακον ἀθανασίας and a lieutenant of the divine physician, a bringer of mercy, healing, forgiveness, and strength. No wonder lava streams of rage erupt and keep flowing. I would like to reflect on the example of one such eruption.

On Monday 28 May 2018, four days after the Irish referendum on abortion, John Waters wrote a piece for the online edition of *First Things* entitled 'Ireland: An Obituary'. In it, Waters lets loose his grief with the cadences of an ancient bard. He shows kinship with the Hebrew prophets too: 'If you would like to visit a place where the symptoms of the sickness of our time are found near their furthest limits, come to Ireland. Here you will see a civilisation in free-fall, seeking with every breath to deny the existence of a higher authority, a people that has now sentenced itself not to look upon the Cross of Christ lest it be haunted by His rage and sorrow'. Do we take seriously the 'rage and sorrow' of Christ? He is, after all, the Lord who will come again to judge the living and the dead – with mercy, yes, but also with truth.

Waters reflects on the brutal nature of the judicial change

effected by the repeal. The Irish Constitution used to say that it 'acknowledges the right to life of the unborn and, with due regard to the equal right to life of the mother, guarantees in its laws to respect, and, as far as practicable, by its laws to defend and vindicate that right'. That paragraph stood to be deleted, to be replaced by one stating coolly that 'provision may be made by law for the regulation or termination of pregnancy'. The right to life of the unborn was swept away, a child in the womb reduced, in Waters's phrase, to 'the mere chattel of her mother'.

There would be much to say about this legislative change. My purpose, however, is to home in on what Waters says about the sentiment that provoked it – for it concerns not only Ireland but all of Europe, and even the whole world. Waters sets out the stakes: 'For the first time in history, a nation has voted to strip the right to life from the unborn. The victims of this dreadful choice will be the most defenceless, those entirely without voice or words. This is the considered verdict of the Irish people, not – as elsewhere – an edict of the elites, imposed by parliamentary decree or judicial fiat. The Irish people are now the happy ones who dash their own children against the rocks [see Psalm 137.9].'

This is a passionate expostulation – a confessional statement, not political analysis. Still, the popular (and populist) nature of the Irish campaign and vote should make us think, for a landslide of this order is not, and cannot be, simply a positive option for agendas of women's lib and political correctness. Such a change bears the hallmark of anger. It is clear at whom the rage is directed. As Waters observes, 'The leveraging of antipathy towards Catholicism is a core element of the pro-abortion strategy.' Much of the vote seems to have been made as an act of spite, a way of spitting in the face of the Church and her pastors. It is a weird but not uncommon syndrome: rebellion against authority through self-harm. How has such fearful fury been stirred up?

Alas, the answer is at hand. The collapse of the Church's credibility not just in Ireland but worldwide has been massive. Ongoing revelations of abuse – abuse of power, abuse of status, sexual and violent abuse – have driven large segments of the Irish nation, and of many other nations, to look on the Church with revulsion, and so to wish to cast off the Catholic 'yoke', to reject a Catholic identity and, as a way of filling the void, to embrace a radically secularist agenda. The Church's discreet presence in the run-up to the Irish referendum can only be understood against this background: There was a sense abroad that anything the Church might say would just make matters worse, that the only course of action was, to paraphrase Isaiah, to go inside, lock the door, and wait for the wrath to pass (Isaiah 26.20).

This is a sorry state for us as Catholics to be in; no, it's worse than sorry: it is abominable. What can we say about the fact that the repeal of the eighth amendment was greeted with music and dancing in the streets? It sends a chill down one's spine to think that such a decision was in large measure an act of defiance. But for the rise of the spirit of defiance, which is not unjustified, the Church must answer; *we* must answer.

We are understandably keen to insist that there is another side to the coin. We invoke the many holy priests and religious we have known, the great good the Church has done and keeps doing, the suffering of those whose lives are wrecked by false accusations of misconduct. These are valid points. But the fact remains that abuse and infidelity have been epidemic, and not just in Ireland. One has the sense of being surrounded by time bombs as country after country reveals dossiers of pain and shame, with uncannily similar patterns of predatory behaviour. *Sauvé* calls these patterns 'systemic'. The density and reach of the dark shadow are immense. It is likely that this past half-century, which at its outset was greeted as the dawn of a new Pentecost, will be remembered as a time of apostasy. I am not trying to be unnecessarily apocalyptic. But it matters to call a spade a spade, so to identify the task which is cut out for us.

For of course we have work to do! I am convinced it is crucial to read this crisis from a theological perspective, and to formulate a theological response. On a practical level, much has already been done, thank God. It is painful but good to map the extent of abuse. Care for victims is essential. Perpetrators of abuse must answer for their deeds. Juridical and canonical reforms to ensure the efficacy of due process are good. It is good to have clear safeguarding procedures. It is good that we have found words to express a corruption that for too long spread silently. Still, if we are to deal with this crisis as believers, more is called for. For we do not face only a legacy of crime; we face a legacy of sin.

Sin, we know, can be forgiven. The Church has always taught, in consonance with Scripture, that God is swift to pardon. Each day the Eucharist is offered 'for the forgiveness of sins'. The fact that a sin has been pardoned does not, though, remove the hurt caused by sin, whether to the sinner or to those affected by the consequence of sin. There may still be a need for reparation and cleansing, whether in this life or in the next. Theology speaks austerely of the 'temporal punishment due to sins already forgiven'. Personally, I find it helpful to think in terms of the 'wages of sin'. We know what they stand for from experience – how a sin committed leaves a wound in our soul, a wound on which we need to keep pouring the balm of God's mercy. The graver the sin, the more infectious and slow-healing the wound.

To be a Catholic today is, I'd say, to live within a huge, unclean, ulcerating wound that cries out for healing. Who is claiming this wound, holding it before God so that, eventually, health may be restored? To explain what I mean by this question, let me draw a parallel to the early nineteenth century. In the wake of the French Revolution and the horrors committed in its name, Catholic France fell to its knees in a prayer of reparation. The great monument to this surging remorse is the basilica of Montmartre, dedicated to the Sacred Heart. In its dome you can read, in letters of gold, this dedication: *Sacratissimo Cordi Iesu Gallia poenitens et devota et grata.* 'To the Most Sacred Heart of Jesus from France penitent, devoted, and grateful.'

The basilica was built as a penitential pledge, a space dedicated to uninterrupted prayer before the Blessed Sacrament, to call Christ's Eucharistic grace down upon a broken nation. What the basilica represents outwardly was lived as an interior, secret reality by countless souls. We shall never understand the resurgence of religious life after the revolution, nor the fervour of nineteenth-century mysticism, if we lose this aspect out of sight. Saint Paul's mysterious words about 'completing what is lacking in Christ's afflictions' (Colossians 1.24) was perceived as a personal call by many.

The saving sacrifice was made on Calvary once for all. It is perfect. But it is not ended. It unfolds within the Church, the Body of Christ, by way of a real presence. Pascal wrote in the *Pensées*, 'Christ remains in agony until the end of time. That isn't a time to be slumbered away.' Many good Christians assumed their share in the task of repairing – through Christ, in him, and with him – the damage wrought by others.

To us, this may seem terribly passé, even a touch embarrassing. The only echo we hear on a regular basis might occur at Benediction, if we recite the Divine Praises composed in 1797 by the Italian Jesuit Father Luigi Felici as a way of making reparation for sacrilege. We should not, though, take this kind of piety lightly. While it did occasionally assume bizarre forms, it rested on solid foundations. Before sin is 'taken away', it has to be assumed and borne. That is the meaning of the cross, which Christ calls us to share by means of a mystery embedded in the structure of the Eucharist. The victorious Lamb is inseparable from the Lamb of sacrifice, the Lamb who bears the sin of the world.

Earlier this autumn, I visited Poland. I was struck by a recurrent motif in that country's sacred art: Again and again I came across representations of the humiliated Christ chained to the pillar in Pilate's *praetorium*, awaiting the lashes of the whip. This same motif played an important role in the second conversion of Teresa of Ávila when, in her forties, she came to see with her heart what she had always known with her mind: the overwhelming weight borne by the Son of God when he suffered 'for our sake'. It is a motif we could profitably rediscover in our time, for our time.

May I share an intimate conviction? I think there is an immense work of bearing to be done in the Church today. I think this bearing, consciously and freely assumed, is a precondition for healing. It belongs above all to us who, as priests and religious, live close to the heart of the Church, which is Christ's heart, cruelly hurt by sin. But it is not ours alone.

Are we willing to take our share of it, for Christ's love's sake? Is our heart alert, open, vulnerable enough to hear the cry of the poor and feel the pain of it? Do we share Christ's 'rage and sorrow' in the face of outrages committed against his little ones? These are urgent questions if, in the renewal we badly need, we wish to maintain the vertical axis of the Church's life.

And what is the Church without a vertical axis? A humanitarian coffee morning, no more – which is an excellent enterprise on its own terms, but hardly a phenomenon that renews and orients our lives, kindles our love, fortifies our hope, purifies our joy, and forms in us courage and peace in the face of death. Life – and death – in Christ doesn't drop from the sky. It needs to be striven for valiantly. The Son of God became man, not to hand out sweetmeats, but to redeem the world. When we look at the world today, it is clear that this work is still sorely needed. Whether the healing potential of the salvific mystery will show itself effective in our time depends in no small part on us, whom Christ calls to live as members of his Body – on how we exercise stewardship of the grace entrusted to us, to enable it to spread.

The New Testament culminates in a majestic description of how, from the throne of the Lamb, the river of the water of life flows out towards the ends of the earth. The river is surrounded by shoots of the tree of life, whose fruit is unfailing and whose leaves are 'for the healing of the nations' (Revelation 22:1ff.). Will we let our living and our dying be a watercourse along which Christ's healing may spread, to reach the desert, death-infected places of our world and of human hearts? The Seer of Patmos ended his book with a clear 'Amen'. Let's make that, likewise, our final note.

6

'Be Holy!': The Scandal of Sanctity

Holiness is a notion we struggle to make sense of now. Confronted with claims to holiness, we instinctively seek to discredit them. The assumption of counterfeit runs deep. To be 'holier-than-thou' is to bask in a self-assigned, self-satisfied sense of superiority that reeks sourly of hypocrisy. If we exclaim of someone 'What a saint!', it is usually to point out some variety of blatant and absurd pharisaical display.

I have occasion to observe popular responses to 'holiness' close at hand. Norway's patron saint, Saint Olav, was killed in 1030. The millennium of his martyrdom draws near inexorably. The government has announced a 'national jubilee' cast as a grand hoorah for our nation, abstracting the protagonist as far as possible. That a modern, secular, multicultural state struggles to frame a response to a Catholic saint is understandable. What is striking, though, is that insofar as Olav is mentioned at all, it is almost always disapprovingly. He is painted in the grim palette of a Netflix Viking series: rapacious, with horns on his hat and an uncontrolled libido.

The fact that Olav was of royal stock, moving easily in princely courts; that we have gracious poems from his hand, songs of swift horses and blushing maidens; that his baptism shows every sign of having been sincere; that he implemented a Christian code of law that raised up the lowly and cast down the proud; that he was known for cheerful kindness; that his cult, upon his defeat in battle, spread fast worldwide; that Christians pilgrimaged secretly to his shrines for centuries after the Reformers had sternly outlawed such practice – all this is pooh-poohed as irrelevant.

At stake is not the relative attractiveness or merit of a particular human destiny. I believe it is the category of 'holiness' as such that causes scandal. That it should be so makes sense. Nowadays we like to project an image of ourselves to the world on the basis of self-affirmation, expecting others to greet it with a Hallelujah chorus. If I admit 'holiness' into my conceptual vocabulary – that is, if I admit the possibility that a human life can be profoundly and durably transformed – who is to say I couldn't, and shouldn't, change *my* life? The thought is uncomfortable.

Have we lost the very ability to portray uncommon goodness? It would seem so. It is damned hard, now, to write up the lives of saints credibly. To label a biography 'hagiography' is to condemn it as idealised drivel. Even sympathetic accounts fall flat. I think of Shūsaku Endō's novel *A Wonderful Fool* from 1959, an attempt to describe the irruption of holiness into a modern, secular setting. The fool in question, a Frenchman named Gaston, steps off a ship in Yokohama one day to visit his Japanese penpal Takamori. Gaston is like a visitor from another planet. He is kind and generous, yes, but hopelessly unrealistic – a misfit even in his unruly physiognomy. Endō, who was a Catholic and wrote as one, sought, it would seem, to create a character in the mould of the *yurodivy* or holy fool canonised in Russian literature. The result, though, reads like a two-dimensional and rather tedious cartoon.

I thought of Endō's novel recently while watching Alice Rohrwacher's movie from 2018, *Lazzaro Felice*. I love the work of Rohrwacher, who, with a keen eye for societal dysfunction and human quirks, makes work that is at the same time critical and uncynical – a delicate balance to tread. There is poetry in all her films; there is mirth, tenderness, intimations of greatness. Lazzaro, meanwhile, stands apart among her *dramatis personae*, for he is wholly good, moving in shabby society as an unlikely incarnation of prelapsarian bliss, happy to let himself be taunted, used, exploited. By narrative and cinematographic means, Rohrwacher lets us see that Lazzaro transcends common human limitations. For one thing, he stands, unageing, beyond chronology. It also becomes clear that he is one for whom the world as it is has neither space nor time. He is shot dead in a high place of pragmatic transaction, a bank, where people around him fatally misread his pure intentions. Poor, naive, foolish Lazzaro! His bright happiness was too much for crepuscular mankind.

The works I have cited, representative of trends, are secular in form. Whatever their authors' beliefs, they do not set out to be explicitly religious. They are certainly not evangelising. What, then, about the Church? Surely she must be an expert on sanctity? Does she have any luck in portraying the inward essence of holy women and men? Thank God, she has the liturgy, whose texts, poetry, and forms carry a timeless treasury that does convey, to those with eyes to see and ears to hear, compelling testimonies. When it comes to contemporary expression, though, even she struggles. To see what I mean, try putting an altarpiece by Fra Angelico or Cimabue, works that take our breath away by probingly displaying humanity imbued with an otherworldliness that does not estrange but perfects it, next to one of the inexplicably ubiquitous mosaics of Marko Rupnik, whose serialised saints have distorted bodies and empty, lightless eyes. An observation will impose itself: Even officially commissioned and sanctioned representations of holiness tend, now, to presuppose *dissimilarity* from actual, lifelike women and men. Sanctity has come to seem corny, somehow, even slightly sinister.

One of the reasons we are in a rut is this: We have come to think of holiness as behavioural perfectibility. We imagine saints as flawless super-persons: nice to all, always patient, not slurping soup, never uttering invective, never crossing the street on a red light. The mere thought of such a person is intolerable. When we see a life projected according to such criteria, it seems unreal. Sniffing fake news, we are only relieved when revelations are made of embarrassing weaknesses or peccadilloes that cause the whole house, precarious from the start, to come tumbling down.

A glance at the Church's catalogue of canonised saints will explode such a limited view of holiness, of course. To list just a few examples: Saint Jerome, patron saint of biblical scholars, was famous for his prickly temperament and salty tongue; Saint Maria Skobtsova, murdered at Ravensbrück, would in Paris throw back her veiled head and put up her feet puffing cigarettes; Saint John Henry Newman descended into doldrums of self-pity; Saint Catherine of Siena spoke her mind to princes in ways that left crowned and tiaraed heads spinning. The saint is no exsanguine transhuman. No, a true saint shows forth what a human being *is* with luminous intensity. We honour the saints not as pupils in life's school who, by swotting, have learnt at last to recite by rote and follow all the rules; we venerate them as graced, gracious human beings in whom the mystery of God flares up like substantial fire.

In likening holiness to fire, I am not just picking a simile out of thin air. When holiness emerges as a biblical category, it is in connection with fire. The setting is Egyptian, likely in the fifteenth century BC. Moses, the Hebrew adopted son of Pharaoh's daughter – ostensibly an orphan, though nursed by his mother – must flee from Pharaoh. His innate instinct for justice had made him commit deeds that drew the establishment's wrath, setting him explicitly apart as the outsider he always, in his heart of hearts, knew he was. Moses, grown up within the known world's stablest structure of power, had become a nomad, erring in the wilderness while seeking pasture for the flocks of Jethro, his father-in-law, priest of Midian. Out there,

> the angel of the Lord appeared to him in a flame of fire out of a bush; he looked, and the bush was blazing, yet it was not consumed. Then Moses said, 'I must turn aside and look at this great sight, and see why the bush is not burned up.' When the Lord saw that he had turned aside to see, God called to him out of the bush, 'Moses, Moses!' And he said, 'Here I am.' Then he said, 'Come no closer! Remove the sandals from your feet, for the place on which you are standing is holy ground.' He said further, 'I am the God of your father, the God of Abraham, the God of Isaac, and the God of Jacob.' And Moses hid his face, for he was afraid to look at God. (Exodus 3.2–6)

There is much going on in this passage. Moses, thinking himself alone in the desert, is surprised by an angelic presence. The angel is not to be identified with God: he is a messenger, carrying God's word; but thereby he does carry something of God's presence, for God is what he speaks. The angel, we might say, is a being made to cross the ontological gap between eternity and time, charged to be a vehicle of God's self-revelation. What is God? An answer to that question cannot be spoken, but is tentatively shown in the figure of fire that burns without consuming. This fire visits the thorn bush like a guest, beautifully seated within it. The thorn bush sustains this visitation. The meeting of supersubstantial fire and matter draws Moses's attention, making him turn aside from his itinerary, wanting and needing to *see*.

Set on the pursuit of sight, he *hears*. 'God called to him out of the bush'. He called him by name. The twofold 'Moses, Moses!' recalls the 'Abraham, Abraham!' by which God called out on Mount Moriah, having tested Abraham by seeing his willingness to sacrifice Isaac, the son whom he loved, as a burnt offering (Genesis 22.11). It further makes us think of the call 'Jacob, Jacob' resounding in visions of the night when the father of Israel's tribes had learnt that Joseph, thought dead, was alive and expecting him in Egypt (Genesis 46.2). There is a note at once of affection and emphasis in the repetition of the name. It is God's way of saying, 'I *know* you'. He, the maker of all, boundless in his absolute being, knows his creatures particularly and intimately.

It is when Moses responds to this call and says, 'Here I am', that he receives the instruction: 'Come no closer! Remove the sandals from your feet, for the place on which you are standing is holy ground [אַדְמַת־קֹדֶשׁ].' Holiness is introduced into biblical vocabulary as a way of expressing the impact of uncreated Being on creation. The place in which the Lord through his angel appears is transformed; it is no longer a patch of ground like any other. Something of God's otherness rubs off on it, eliciting from man extraordinary comportment. To take off one's shoes is to show reverence. It is also to enable immediacy. Moses is asked to step into the radius of epiphany without a layer between his own self and God's radiance. He must make himself vulnerable to this encounter in order to be changed by it.

There follows an exchange that explicates the purpose of such change. Moses is called into the realm of eternity not just as a reward for private virtue; he is to be an instrument in God's hands for the realisation of a providential plan. Having given through fire an inkling of *what* he is like, God reveals *who* he is with reference to past revelations: 'I am the God of your father, the God of Abraham, the God of Isaac, and the God of Jacob.' This supratemporal, burning Godhead makes himself incrementally known in time. Moses is chosen as a link in the chain of revelation stretching across the patriarchal stories.

Yet he, the intrepid, responds with fear. Why? We can propose a philosophical answer. Man is in himself ephemeral: 'All flesh is like grass and all its glory like the flower of grass. The grass withers, and the flower falls' (1 Peter 1.24; see Isaiah 40.6–7). Faced with the source of Reality, which has no beginning and no end, such a fragile thing recoils, unfit to bear the weight of glory. Moses's fear can be understood as the spontaneous worship later generations would call, precisely, 'fear of God', intending the appropriate response of fallen creatures to God's nearness.

Permit me to propose a further interpretation of Moses's fear. It complements, without contradicting, the one we have considered. Originating with Rabbi Nachum Rabinovitch, it has been cogently expounded by Jonathan Sacks. Sacks sets out from Moses's passion for justice. When Moses saw a slave maltreated, or people fighting, or women ill-treated, he acted; he did not stand around the corner saying, 'Tut!' (Exodus 2.11–18). The sages of Israel tell us that Moses was haunted by the scandal of evil in the world. The thought of innocent suffering, the treading-down of justice and truth, tormented him. Remember the audacity with which he later took the Lord to task when Pharaoh brutalised his Hebrew workforce. Moses told God, 'Since I first came to Pharaoh to speak in your name, he has mistreated this people, and you have done nothing at all to deliver your people' (Exodus 5.23). There is righteous passion here, all right.

Such passion is possible, and licit, in a worldview founded on the notion that justice is structural to the way in which the world is made. Such is the biblical view. Scripture presents the universe as an intelligent *kosmos* in which each part is attuned elegantly to others, a compositional model intended to apply to human society as well. The 'way of the Lord' is 'righteousness and justice'. This principle has been axiomatic since the days of Abraham (Genesis 18.19). What, then, when it does not work out? What can we say faced with the failure of good and the triumph of wickedness, with the tears of orphans, the rage of the oppressed, the terror of the sick and persecuted?

The Bible allows for this perplexity, tracing it to an immanent wound in humanity's constitution that caused the chronicle of our race to originate in fratricide (Psalm 133.1; Genesis 4.8). Indeed, not only does Scripture affirm that circumstances of pain may obtain in our life; it tells us that they are sometimes necessary, that at times evil must be borne patiently by those who are not its agents.

Thereby an economy of salvation and healing works out in history – to our perception, shockingly slowly, but in the eyes of the Lord, for whom a thousand years are like a day, assuredly (2 Peter 3.8). In human affairs there are moments, writes Sacks, 'when we must silence our most human instincts if we are to bring about good in the long run', accepting that not each deliverance is instantaneous and that suffering, an ill in itself, is sometimes purposeful, requisite.

Rabbi Rabinovitch maintained that it was of this that Moses was afraid. Was looking at the face of God not tantamount to seeing history as God sees it? And was this not a proposition whose price was too high? How could Moses 'still be moved by the cry of slaves, the anguish of the oppressed, if he understood its place in the scheme of things, if he knew that it was necessary in the long run?'

> Such knowledge is divine, not human – and to have it means saying goodbye to our most human instincts: compassion, sympathy, identification with the plight of the innocent, the wronged, the afflicted and oppressed. If to look at the face of God is to understand why suffering is sometimes necessary, then Moses was afraid to look – afraid that it would rob him of the one thing he felt in his very bones, the thing that made him the leader he was: his anger at the sight of evil which drove him . . . to intervene in the name of justice.

The God whom Moses met in the bush is called *Elohim*, a name the rabbis associate with God's justice. It took Moses years to integrate the further name revealed in that epiphany: the ineffable *Tetragrammaton*, which Jewish tradition transcribes as *Hashem*, 'the Name', a manifestation of divine compassion. When, later in the story, on and after Sinai, Moses looks fearlessly at God, it is *Hashem* he sees. Whereas God's justice can unsettle our minds, even appear to us cruel, his compassion illumines us in ways that supersede reason, letting us intuit his salvific grace where we cannot grasp it.

To step into the orbit of holiness, to risk sanctification, requires assent to phenomenal tension as we resolve to construct our lives justly while agreeing to be formed by compassion in unsettlingly palpable experiences of, precisely, 'suffering *with*'. For while the world is sick, afflicted with iniquity, there will be pangs of healing to sustain; and humankind is so composed that a part can effectively carry out work on behalf of the whole. In Israel's mature reflection, holiness is an attribute of God. The vision of Isaiah, in which he saw the Lord on a throne surrounded by angels calling out, 'Holy, holy, holy [קָדוֹשׁ קָדוֹשׁ קָדוֹשׁ] is the Lord of hosts' (Isaiah 6.3), constitutes a paradigm. Human beings perceive holiness insofar as they glimpse something of God's glory; they are made holy, meanwhile, by configuration to the Holy and Perfect One, who is compassionate, in the midst of realities racked by imperfection. For Christians, this incursion of glory into trauma is crystallised in Christ's Incarnation. The Incarnation renews our nature, opening it to communion with God, letting us hear the cross-shaped call 'Be holy!' as one we can follow without presumption. It spells a broadening of being and mind intended and worked on divine purpose. To see this process at work in a human being is to sense something of what Moses sensed at the bush: the bewildering presence of the Holy One in the here and now.

An example of sanctification which has long haunted me is that of Takashi Nagai, born near Hiroshima in 1908, when Japan, after centuries of isolationism, had catapulted itself into modernity.

Takashi, now declared by the Church a Servant of God, was formed in the Japanese classics, whose limpid poetry he loved; at the same time, he was drawn to new science. He studied medicine (from German manuals) in Nagasaki, where circumstances of health and chance got him interested in radiology. He would become one of Japan's best experts in this field in which he practised assiduously as a clinician, exposing himself to rays that would provoke severe leukaemia. He spent two periods of military service in China, first in 1933, then for three years from 1937 during the Second Sino-Japanese War, appalled at the brutality he saw, but strengthened in his humanitarian ethos.

This ethos, at first quite secular, was little by little enlightened from another source. As a youth, Takashi had spurned faith. He reconsidered his position at his mother's deathbed. An urgent telegram from his father summoned him home in late March 1930. He found his mother Tsune, a descendant of samurai, immobilised and mute after a cerebral haemorrhage. She spent her last strength awaiting Takashi's arrival. Just minutes after he had come to her, she expired. He later wrote,

> I rushed to her bedside. She was still breathing. She looked fixedly at me, and that is how the end came. My mother in that last penetrating gaze knocked down the ideological framework I had constructed. . . . Her eyes spoke to mine, and with finality, saying: 'Your mother now takes leave in death, but her living spirit will be beside her little one, Takashi!' I who was so sure that there was no such thing as a spirit was now told otherwise; and I could not but believe. My mother's eyes told me that the human

spirit lives on after death. All this was by way of intuition, an intuition carrying conviction.

Many people might be pierced by such intuition for an instant, then let it go. That was no option for Takashi, whose rigorous intellect would not permit him to abandon a loose thread of such import. Picking it up, he began to spool it.

He was given two leads. The first was Blaise Pascal, the seventeenth-century philosopher whom Takashi had discovered while studying literature at school. Pascal's aphoristic style, familiar to an ear attuned to Japanese poetry, pleased him. He later learnt that Pascal was also a scientist. Takashi procured a copy of his *Pensées*, a school of metaphysical reasoning and Christian perception. The book confirmed him in his compassion for mankind, but added a challenging dimension by stating, 'Our wretchedness is that of a dispossessed king'. Takashi might assimilate notions of grace, first innocence, sin, and forgiveness, but his scientist's mind balked at Pascal's insistence that faith is a suprarational gift from God, necessitating prayer.

What prayer is he learnt from living persons. The year following his mother's death, he took lodgings in Nagasaki with a family sprung from the stock of Christians who trace their faith back to Saint Francis Xavier. From the outset, Japanese authorities had viewed Christianity hostilely. Martin Scorsese's 2016 film *Silence*, based on a book by Endō, has made the ensuing cultural battle well known. It shows how, in the 1630s, while Pascal was an adolescent, European clergy in Japan were crucified and the Church was forced underground, there to become a movement of 'hidden Christians'. This movement, concentrated in the region of Urakami, just north of Nagasaki, had formed the faith of Takashi's landlords, the Moriyamas. Several waves of persecution rose during two and a half centuries of Tokugawa rule. A final campaign took place upon the Meiji Restoration in 1868. Takashi knew several survivors of the prison camps that, between 1868 and 1873, produced heroic martyrs. The faith he came to know in person had been purified by fire.

This cursory account enables us to trace four decisive factors in Takashi's Christian journey: the death of his mother in 1930; immersion in Pascal; exposure to the horrors of war; then, acquaintance with the Urakami Christians. Takashi was baptised in Urakami's new cathedral in June 1934. Two months later, he married the Moriyamas' daughter Midori, a woman of great inward and outward strength.

During the decade that followed, Takashi's life assumed adult consistency. It was shaped, like any life, by joy and pain. He and Midori had three children. One died in infancy. Three years of conscription in China taught Takashi to pray. His research in radiology prospered. The more he immersed himself in science, he found that, contrary to his first assumption, it confirmed his faith. 'On one occasion, while studying a kidney case and looking at the brilliant formation of urine crystals, he "felt a great urge to kneel". He saw "that a laboratory could be the same as the cell of a monk"'. In June 1945, Takashi, long exposed to powerful radiation, was found to be in an advanced stage of blood cancer. He was peacefully reconciled to his mortality, but as unprepared as anyone for the force with which death would sweep over Nagasaki on 9 August, when the A-bomb was dropped on the city.

We know that the bomb was intended for another location, some 200 kilometers to the north. Weather conditions and a technical issue in the carrying plane made this target unreachable. The pilot homed in instead on Urakami. Takashi has described what happened just past 11, when, at work in the hospital, he saw a blinding light:

> A giant hand seemed to grab me and hurl me ten feet. Fragments of glass flew about like leaves in a whirlwind. My eyes were open, and I had a glimpse of the outside – planks, beams, clothing were doing a weird dance in the air. . . . The giant invisible hand had gone berserk and was smashing everything in the office. Various objects fell on top of me while I listened to strange noises like mountains rumbling back and forth. Then came pitch darkness, as if the reinforced concrete hospital were an express train that had just rushed headlong into a tunnel. I had felt no pain as yet, but panic gripped my heart when I heard crackling flames and sniffed acrid smoke.

Takashi heard himself say, 'Midori, it's the end; I'm dying.' When he came to, what struck him was the silence. He was alive, but the world seemed dead, still, wholly burnt. Then, outside, he noticed pitiful shapes crawling about, their bodies swollen, their skin peeling as they joined in a sepulchral chorus: 'I am burning! Water!' With a handful of colleagues, he attended to this scene of devastation, caring for mangled bodies, trying to keep afflicted minds from surrender to madness.

There was evening and morning, evening again, then another morning. On 11 August, Takashi could at last return to what had been his home. There was nothing there but ash. In the midst of it, he found a heap of bones. It was Midori, holding in her right hand a melted lump that, by a fragment of the chain and the still visible cross, Takashi identified as her rosary. He has written of how he buried her, asking forgiveness for the ways in which his love had been imperfect, only to hear her voice in his heart saying, 'No forgive *me*; I ask for forgiveness'. In a strange sweetness of reconciliation that transcended calculable culpability, Takashi buried his wife.

Sick with cancer, sustaining the impact of the bomb, Takashi's body gave in. By September, haemorrhaging incurably, he accepted that the end had come. He took leave of his children, who had been absent from Nagasaki on 9 August. While auto-diagnosing the rapid breathing that heralds final agony, an inspiration came to him to pray to Father Maximilian Kolbe. We think of Kolbe now as the Martyr of Auschwitz. Before the dramatic final part of his life, however, he spent long years as a missionary in Japan. To Takashi, he was an old acquaintance: He had x-rayed Father Maximilian for tuberculosis. Takashi did pray, though. To his colleagues' astonishment, his bleeding stopped. Takashi's mother-in-law, having no idea what was going on in Takashi's mind and heart, gave him water from a nearby Lourdes grotto, one that Father Kolbe had built. Again, against the odds, Takashi had been snatched from death's jaw. He knew it was for a purpose.

His life thenceforth carried a supernatural sheen all the more impressive for shining within resolute attachment to present, material reality. He devoted himself to the rebuilding of Nagasaki. He built a hut where his house had stood, determined to make this wasteland reflourish. He must live right there, he said, to contemplate the meaning of what had taken place. Of this contemplation he had occasion to speak on 23 November 1945, when Nagasaki's bishop offered an open-air Mass for the dead. Well in advance, he had asked Takashi to speak on behalf of the laity. What could a man possibly say in such conditions, to people who had lost everything?

Three considerations merged in Takashi's mind. The first was a story he had heard of girls from the convent school of Junshin, where Midori had taught. After the blast, horribly burnt, they were heard singing a hymn learnt at school: 'Mary, Mother! I offer myself to you, body, soul, and spirit!' This story conjured up for Takashi the image from Revelation of the Lamb, slaughtered for the world's redemption, followed by white-robed, chanting virgins. He wrote a poem:

> Maidens like white lilies
> Consumed in the burning flames
> As a whole burnt sacrifice
> And they were singing.

A second consideration was this: Just as the bomb was dropped on Nagasaki, the Supreme Council of War was in session in Tokyo. Many generals opposed surrender. The council was deadlocked. Talks continued throughout the day. At midnight, the emperor cut through and declared capitulation. At midnight, likewise, Urakami's smouldering cathedral burst into full flames and was consumed. The third consideration sprang from what Takashi had learnt from the descendants of the 'hidden Christians': that Urakami was irrigated by the blood of martyrs.

On that late-November day, at Mass, in the context of Christ's saving sacrifice, among ruins, Takashi rose unkempt before his fellow citizens and asked, 'Is there not a profound relationship between the annihilation of Nagasaki and the end of the war? Was not

Nagasaki the chosen victim, the lamb without blemish, slain as a whole burnt offering on an altar of sacrifice, atoning for the sins of all the nations during World War II?' Several in the congregation, appalled to hear the carnage spoken of as providence, responded with anger. Takashi, though, went on, broadening the perspective:

> We are inheritors of Adam's sin, of Cain's sin. He killed his brother. Yes, we have forgotten we are God's children. We have turned to idols and forgotten love. Hating one another, killing one another, joyfully killing one another! At last the evil and horrific conflict came to an end, but mere repentance was not enough for peace. We had to offer a stupendous sacrifice. . . . Happy are those who weep; they shall be comforted. We must walk the way of reparation, ridiculed, whipped, punished for our crimes, sweaty and bloody. But we can turn our mind's eyes to Jesus carrying his Cross up the hill to Calvary. The Lord has given, the Lord has taken away. Blessed be the name of the Lord. Let us be *thankful* that Nagasaki was chosen for the whole burnt sacrifice. Let us be thankful that through this sacrifice, peace was granted to the world, and religious freedom to Japan.

When he finished, the silence was as deep as after the explosion. People needed time to absorb the mere possibility of such a point of view. Takashi did not loudly canvas for it. But he sought to put it into comprehensible words. He turned to writing. After producing a scientific treatise on the condition of A-bomb victims, he adopted a different genre. This enterprise grew out of a madcap scheme to unearth a bell from the ruins of Urakami's cathedral. The southern bell tower had collapsed into itself. There was a chance its bell might still be intact. In Advent 1945, Takashi and a few friends dug for it. They uncovered it on Christmas Eve, set up a tripod of logs, hung the bell, then rang the Angelus at 6 p.m. The Christians of Urakami were amazed to hear this familiar, well-loved bell proclaim, 'The Word was made flesh, and dwelt among us.' Takashi's first popular book, *The Bells of Nagasaki*, was born of that sound. It stated that no human devilry can undermine God's serene, redemptive plan.

First ridiculed as defeatist, Takashi was gradually hailed as an agent in the reconstruction of Japan. By the end of 1948, everyone was reading him. *The Bells of Nagasaki* was made into a film. He told survivors that they had work to do; that nothing is in vain; that realities impervious to the question 'Why?' may release their secret when asked 'What for?' At the requiem in the ruins, he cited Job. Like Job, he had known unconscionable loss. He had looked into the abyss, yet refused to despair, affirming that God is surely present *in* his apparent absence. Perceiving light in darkness, he acquired a new sense of who God, the righteous and compassionate, is, thereby seeing – 'My eyes shall behold, and not another' (Job 19.27) – the emergence of a new heaven, a new earth. What Job glimpsed in figures, Takashi scrutinised in the light of the Word's Incarnation, a joyful but unsentimental mystery whose emblem is, and remains, the cross. He would say, 'Let us climb the Mountain of the Beatitudes', then remind himself and others that it arises out of the valley of the shadow of death. For unless 'you've looked into the eyes of menacing death and felt its hot breath, you can't help another rise from the dead and taste anew the joy of being alive.' Joy, marked by zany humour, radiated from him until he expired on 1 May 1951. Before he died, he used savings to have a thousand cherry blossom trees planted in Urakami.

Takashi Nagai was no wonderful fool like Gaston or Lazzaro. He was a lucid, observant man. His holiness was not at odds with the world of terror and tears in which he lived; it articulated that world. That makes him an exemplar for our times of menace and widespread anguish. Not only do conceptual, cultural, and political structures fall around us like dominoes; we have lost a consensual understanding of what man is, so have trouble sustaining society. To proffer the biblical vocation to holiness as a response to such a predicament amounts to more than saying that we must do our very best to be very, very good. It calls on us to remove our shoes and step, vulnerable, into the orbit of God's fiery presence, to be cleansed by it in order to become that fire's bearers. To respond to this call is risky. It may involve sacrifice. But it will burst barriers that, in a purely pragmatic existence, suffocate us. It will release breath and joy. Each woman or man will live this process differently, but certain traits will be constant, criteria of authenticity. I think of Pascal's famous *Mémorial*, his testament to an illumination received after vehement searching, a statement so vital to him that he carried it on him always, having the text of it sewn into his clothes. The *Mémorial* is dated 23 November 1653. That same day, 292 years later, Takashi Nagai exegeted the conflagration of Nagasaki in a public address at a requiem. The coincidence will not have been lost on that assiduous reader of Pascal. The *Mémorial* begins with a monosyllabic exclamation: *Feu!*, 'Fire!' It goes on:

> GOD of Abraham, GOD of Isaac, GOD of Jacob
> not of the philosophers and of the learned.
> Certitude. Certitude. Affection. Joy. Peace.
> GOD of Jesus Christ.

> My God and your God.
> Your GOD will be my God.
> Forgetfulness of the world and of everything,
> except GOD.
> He is only found by the ways taught in the Gospel.
> Grandeur of the human soul.
> Righteous Father, the world has not known you, but I have known you.

'I came', said our Lord Jesus Christ, 'to bring fire to the earth, and how I wish it were already kindled!' (Luke 12.49). His aspiration concerns us directly. In the *Sayings of the Desert Fathers*, we find this story of a conversation between two old friends: 'Abba Lot went to Abba Joseph and said to him, "Abba, as far as I can I say my little office, I fast a little, I pray and meditate, I live in peace and as far as I can, I purify my thoughts. What else can I do?" Then the old man stood up and stretched his hands towards heaven. His fingers became like ten lamps of fire and he said to him, "If you will, you can become fire."' This is the scandal and challenge presented to us, before which we must position ourselves with freedom. Let us be mindful, simply, that the answer we give does not concern ourselves alone. The call to each is given for the sake of all. The wholehearted yes of one, even if it be hidden, can bring about the comfort of multitudes.

7

Synodality and Holiness

In April 2023, I was privileged to address the General Chapter of the Benedictine Congregation of Solesmes. The assembly had asked me to reflect on the theme of 'Synodality and Holiness'. I was perplexed at first. I had not thought of synodality in terms of holiness. True, we have recently heard the word used such a lot that we have come to think it has a bearing on everything, though in terms of an essential bond it is usually associated not with an eschatological ideal, but with a process of government linked to the motions of an ecclesiastical body: Vatican II.

Observers have argued that the now ongoing synod's vision is like the overflowing of the council's cup. Cardinal Grech, the synod's secretary general, has been more cautious, conceding that the word 'synodality' is absent from the council's documents but submitting it arises therefrom in the manner of a dream. If we struggle to configure the dream, it may be because 'synodality' is protean, prone, as another authority has pointed out, to be 'dynamic' rather than 'static', like the sea.

Not all are born sailors. Some face the waves anxiously, seeking a fixed point, a constellation in the sky to steer by. For such, the category of holiness is helpful. The commission I received this spring taught me that. It led me to adjust my perspective and perceive the sought-for bridge uniting the synod's work now to the council's vision and teaching. For as far as holiness is concerned, the council was wonderfully explicit. The fifth chapter of the great constitution on the Church, *Lumen gentium*, set holiness as the note by which all the Church's instruments must ever be tuned. Christ, we are reminded, 'loved the Church as His bride, delivering Himself up for her. He did this that He might sanctify her'. Only insofar as we consent to be sanctified in Christ will we correspond to our Christian purpose and foster 'a more human manner of living' in this world, whose descent into inhumanity terrifies. The council insists that each state of life has a holiness proper to it. Pursuit of it will call for sacrifice. The witness of the martyrs is evoked. The summing-up is almost incredibly bold: 'All the faithful of Christ are invited to strive for the holiness and perfection of their own proper state. Indeed they have an obligation to so strive.' From this obligation a practical consequence is drawn: 'Let all then have care that they guide aright their own deepest sentiments of soul'.

Deep sentiments of soul are now at stake. It seems timely to weigh them against this summons. We might do so by reviewing the motif of synodality first in the Old Testament, then in the New, in order to ask how best we might apply it to our lives – how it might lead us together to the goal we seek: holiness.

SYNODALITY IN THE OLD TESTAMENT

Let us first clarify terminology. The etymology of *synodos* has been rehearsed ad nauseam: *hodos* is Greek for 'a way'; *syn* means 'with'.

A *synodos* is a way pursued in fellowship, a journey shared. A journey, it's worth noting at the outset, presupposes a goal. The ascetic tradition is scathing about pilgrims who walk round and round. Saint Benedict saw the type of such circularity, the *gyrovague*, as the ultimate loser. For biblically minded people, the notion of the 'way' evokes strong associations. We know from Saint Luke that the Church in apostolic times was called 'the Way' (Acts 9.2). Christ declared himself to be '*the* way' (John 14.6). That is the Way to follow. Its goal is clear. In the high priestly prayer, Christ prayed, 'Father, I desire that those also, whom you have given me, may be with me where I am, to see my glory' (John 17.24). The human race's call since the beginning has been to be with the Father's beloved Son, the Image of God (Colossians 1.15) in whom we were created, now and for ever.

A degree of synodality is implicit in God's act of creation: 'Let us make humankind in our image, according to our likeness' (Genesis 1.26). To realise our iconic potential, to become like God, is the purpose of our being. Such movement is not accomplished in isolation. After the creation of Eve, man and woman were to be, in consecrated union, 'one flesh' (Genesis 2.24), oriented towards one another in complementarity. The dynamic is applicable more broadly. It is meeting the gaze of another that reveals me to myself, enabling me to understand and develop myself in communion.

The account of original communion is followed by the story of the Fall. It reveals a darker side of synodality: 'When the woman saw that the tree was good for food, and that it was a delight to the eyes, and that the tree was to be desired to make one wise, she took of its fruit and ate; and she also gave some to her husband, who was with her, and he ate. Then the eyes of both were opened, and they knew that they were naked' (Genesis 3.6–7). Collusion resulted in the death of innocence. The other, familiarly reassuring just a moment ago, was reduced to a stranger, at once attractive and fearful.

Scripture qualifies the action provoking the Fall as 'sin', a death-dealing loss of direction. One result of sin is the more or less deliberate will to entice others into my forlornness, which seems to me now, owing to a numbing of consciousness, as reality itself, my *milieu vital*. The thought of remaining alone in it is unbearable. A call to walk synodally away from a freely owned dependence on God is made explicit in the project of Babel. People said to each other, 'Come, let us build ourselves a city, and a tower with its top in the heavens, and let us make a name for ourselves; otherwise we shall be scattered abroad upon the face of the whole earth' (Genesis 11.4). Their desire was to maintain a coherent assembly, to create a societal model attractive enough to unite all humankind. Their criteria were self-destructive, although they did not see it. The project was sabotaged by the Lord himself.

The vocation of Abraham, our father in faith, was synodal. Having heard God's call, he took 'his wife Sarai and his brother's son Lot . . . and the persons whom they had acquired in Haran', and set forth to go to the land of Canaan (Genesis 12.5). At first, it went well enough. As long as the journey's destination is remote, susceptible of idealisation, synodality does not pose major challenges; travellers envisage the nature of the trip as they please. When the journey's end approaches, when questions arise of dividing territory, tensions arise. The possessions of Abram and Lot were such that 'the land could not support both of them living together' (Genesis 13.6). They split. 'Separate yourself from me', said Abraham. 'If you take the left hand, then I will go to the right' (Genesis

13.9). This story helps us relinquish simplistic notions of synodality. If one does not have the same finality in mind, the same image of a paradise to restore, a centrifugal force will make itself felt. Unity, ever vulnerable, will then be liable to break.

This tendency is at work in the story of Israel's exodus from Egypt, which structures our preparation for Easter each year. Moses, Aaron, Miriam, and a handful of initiates, prepared by providence, had a lucid view of the reasons why they must get out of Egypt and find the promised land. The synodal assembly at large was more pragmatically minded. These folks desired a better quality of life, diversion, recognition. Such aspirations are legitimate, but insufficient to preserve unity in forward movement for a variegated crowd, a *vulgus promiscuum innumerabile*, to cite Jerome's memorable rendering of Exodus 12.38. We are given to understand that the 'countless mixed crowd' had elements of both vulgarity and promiscuity. Its integration into the exodus marked the beginning of an account of multiple conflicts, dissensions, and breakaways.

Anyone with the time and inclination might pursue this reading of the synodal motif through the historical and prophetic writings. What we are left with is an Old Testament perspective on synodality which cannot be called cynical, for each page of Scripture is redolent with hope; it is simply realistic. This is useful. To proceed together towards holiness, towards an encounter with the Holy One, we must follow a royal road that is sometimes narrow.

SYNODALITY IN THE NEW TESTAMENT

The Gospel passage most commonly referred to in synodal texts is the story of the wanderers to Emmaus. It is sublime, offering ever new layers of meaning. We might equally well perform a reading in a synodal key of the call to Mary or the Apostles, to Mary Magdalene or Paul. Thereby we could learn much about what it means to walk in companionship with the Son of God. It is his presence, after all, that makes up the criterion for synodal authenticity.

I am drawn to a more discreet synodal narrative in the New Testament, the testimony of a man who came to faith almost despite himself; who followed Jesus at a distance, though without losing sight of him; who stayed faithful to the end, though remaining in the shadow.

I speak of Nicodemus. Nicodemus, 'a leader of the Jews', turns up in the third chapter of the fourth Gospel. 'He came to Jesus by night' (John 3.2), an approach emblematic of our times, whose faith often has a nocturnal character. Nicodemus poses pondered questions. He is reflective, serious, seeking real answers to real problems. In this respect, too, he represents the present mood.

Nicodemus wants to be heard yet is able to listen attentively. Here we touch a raw nerve. On the whole, we are not very good, now, at listening. We are collectively afflicted with logorrhoea, prone to inattention and selective deafness. This is also true within the Church, in synodal discourse. Everyone has something to say. Everyone expects to be heard. But are we willing to listen to what the Lord says, then to heed firm in faith, strong in resolve, freely and trustfully?

Jesus's conversation with Nicodemus touches God's self-revelation. It tells us that it is possible to live a life saturated by God's Spirit. It speaks of God's philanthropy, which leads him to empty himself that we might live, an example we are bidden to imitate; it posits eternal life as the one worthy goal of man's pilgrimage on earth; it stresses the freedom we possess to choose between life and death, light and darkness, a freedom for which we must one day answer before God. On that day we must give an account in person for choices we have made, even though they may have been swayed by synodal energies.

Having heard and received Jesus's teaching, Nicodemus recedes back into the night. He embodies a splendid text in Isaiah: 'My soul yearns for you in the night, my spirit within me earnestly seeks you. For when your judgements are in the earth, the inhabitants of the world learn righteousness' (26.9). Nicodemus is one who truly waits for God's judgement to shine on earth.

We encounter him again at a meeting of officials, during which high priests and Pharisees seek to eliminate Jesus. Nicodemus protests, 'Our law does not judge people without first giving them a hearing to find out what they are doing, does it?' (John 7.51). To walk with Jesus and create about him synodal fellowship, we must weigh his words and deeds, seeking their significance and grounding ourselves in his salvific epiphany without giving in to passing views, prejudices, and expectations.

Nicodemus's third appearance in the Gospel is by Jesus's tomb. Clearly he has followed the Crucifixion at a distance. Now, when the disciples grieve over their friend, he draws close, bringing 'a mixture of myrrh and aloes, weighing about a hundred pounds' (John 19.39). The Christians of the Middle Ages meditated at length on this scene. They saw in Nicodemus one who had pierced the mystery of the Passion, who had embraced it, and could therefore communicate it to others. A tradition arose that attributed works of art, moving representations of the Crucified, to Nicodemus. He was considered the creator of both the Holy Face of Lucca and the Batlló Crucifix. It is significant, surely, that our medieval forbears found him apt to be a sculptor, master of a tactile art, forming what he had seen with his eyes, touched with his hands (see 1 John 1.1). Without needing to debate the veracity of such ascription, we can recognise in it perennial symbolic validity and value.

Nicodemus is, I submit, an example for us who strive synodally to be true disciples and seekers after holiness. Why? He stays away from facile polemics and theatrical gestures. Still, he follows the Lord wherever he goes. When he is needed, he offers his service and volunteers his friendship to the community. He shows us what it means to be faithful in the darkness of Good Friday. Contemplating the crucified, entombed Christ, he had wisdom to recognise in desolation something sublime, a glorious, divine revelation. Thus he became an authoritative witness to the Crucified's victory. Truly, this is an attitude the Church needs now.

AND WE?

To be a Christian, a Catholic, today is challenging. There's no two ways about it. Looking around we can be tempted to exclaim with a Psalm: 'O God, the heathen have come into your inheritance; they have defiled your holy temple; they have laid Jerusalem in ruins' (Psalm 79.1 RSV-CE). To be a heathen is to be one who does not truly believe, however much he may carry trappings of faith. We live with the wounds of abuse, which we all hoped would be a matter concerning just our neighbours, not us. Our communities are shrinking. The agonising question 'How long?' presents itself in settings that within living memory seemed unshakable. Trust has been betrayed. Prophets of desolation abound. The spirit of division, rife in society, raises its ugly head in the Church too. There is a peculiar sadness abroad.

And yet this is the day – and night – that the Lord has made and entrusted to us, that it may be for us a time of salvation. How can we, in such a time, live out our vocation to holiness?

First by bearing, at one with the Lamb of God, our part of the weight of the sin of the world, a sin not reducible simply to ungodly acts. This sin stands no less for a worldly lostness chaotically voicing pain that tends towards despair, often lacking an object and for that reason being especially redoubtable. The Lamb of God 'takes away the sins of the world', not by snapping his fingers like a magician, but by *bearing* it. We are called to live as members of his Body.

The faithful who, with Nicodemus, are summoned to prefer light to darkness at all costs (see John 3.18–21) must be ready to bear synodally the weight of night which is the portion of many people now. This presupposes readiness to stay within that night, praying *there*, loving and serving *there*, slowly recognising *there*, even if it be at a distance, the light no darkness can overcome (John 1.5).

Reading and rereading the sources of monasticism, the great Lives (of Antony, Hypatios, and others) that, before Rules were written, indicated the path to life, I am struck by the recurrence of the *topos* of compassion, understood concretely as willingness to 'suffer with'. This is surely a key aspect of the synodal experience: participation, by means of patience, in the redemptive Passion of Christ. This is a time to reflect on what Paul speaks of in a hushed voice to the Colossians: 'In my flesh I complete what is lacking in Christ's afflictions for the sake of his body, that is, the Church' (1.24). It is profoundly significant that the Second Vatican Council, expounding the universal call to holiness, referred explicitly to martyrdom:

Since Jesus, the Son of God, manifested His charity by laying down His life for us, so too no one has greater love than he who lays down his life for Christ and His brothers. From the earliest times, then, some Christians have been called upon — and some will always be called upon — to give the supreme testimony of this love to all men, but especially to persecutors. The Church, then, considers martyrdom as an exceptional gift and as the fullest proof of love. By martyrdom a disciple is transformed into an image of his Master by freely accepting death for the salvation of the world — as well as his conformity to Christ in the shedding of his blood. Though few are presented such an opportunity, nevertheless all must be prepared to confess Christ before men. They must be prepared to make this profession of faith even in the midst of persecutions, which will never be lacking to the Church, in following the way of the cross.

'All *must* be prepared'. Without melodrama, with Christian sobriety charged with good sense, we must own that this call touches us. Likewise we must believe that the messy unpredictability marking any *vulgus promiscuum* making its way in synodal progress, following the path of the commandments, secretly realises a divine melody. I take immense comfort in the confession of a Benedictine nun of the past century, Sister Elisabeth Paule Labat, who intimately knew the vicissitudes and traumas of life while remaining rooted in the freeing, transforming grace of the cross. She articulated her mature insight thus:

> [Growing in wisdom] man will perceive the history of this world in whose battle he is still engaged as an immense symphony

resolving one dissonance by another until the intonation of the perfect major chord of the final cadence at the end of time. Every being, every thing contributes to the unity of that intelligible composition, which can only be heard from within: sin, death, sorrow, repentance, innocence, prayer, the most discreet and the most exalted joys of faith, hope, and love; an infinity of themes, human and divine, meet, flee, and are intertwined before finally melting into one according to a master plan which is nothing other than the will of the Father, pursuing through all things the infallible realisation of its designs.

Holiness is an essential category, not a label attached as a seal to impeccable conduct. Holiness is that which is essentially divine, categorically unlike any quality extant in creation, even the loveliest. The way to holiness is illumined by uncreated light. We must be changed to perceive it. Our eyes, hearts, and senses must be opened; we must step outside our limitations, into a dimension of truth that is of God.

Synodality leading in this direction, configuring us to our crucified and risen Lord, is life-giving, redolent with the sweet perfume of Christ Jesus (2 Corinthians 2.15). Synodality, meanwhile, that encloses us in limited desires and predictions, reducing the purpose of God to our measure, must be treated with great caution.

8

Setting 'Spirituality' Free

If the truth be told, I am sick and tired of the word 'spirituality'. In ordinary parlance, it often carries no definable content. I sometimes think 'spirituality' has become a designation for subjectivised religion freed from dogmas and commandments — and to a large extent from revelation.

In Northern Europe, marked by the Protestant revolutions of the sixteenth century, we tend to subjectivise spiritual things. Just a couple of generations ago, it was common enough to hear people speak about faith on the basis of private notions of 'my god': 'My god isn't this way or that, doesn't do that sort of thing.' It was chiefly a matter of distancing oneself from the concept of the covenant, the biblical idea that God, ruler of all, relates to humankind on the basis of a bilateral testament marked by a number of conditions, that he calls us into a social and theological context marked by obligation. A God who makes demands and seeks to incorporate me into a superior *cosmos* is troublesome.

Talk of 'my god' made transcendence malleable. It set out from the fantasy of omnipotence seeing me as the centre of the universe, surrounding me like a feather duvet. It is an enticing fantasy; but with time it has faded like dew before the ego's sun. Unless I've turned tone-deaf and no longer notice what people are saying, it seems to me that hardly anyone, now, speaks of 'my god'. The very thought of 'god' has been shelved; it presupposes a subjectivity transcending mine. That is currently off-limits. What we believe in these days is 'my spirituality', a tailor-made ensemble of desires, experiences, wishes, and imaginations corresponding to my needs and permitting me to project an idealised image of self. Isn't 'spirituality' often a kind of sublimated narcissism?

The trouble is that 'spirituality' has turned into a word susceptible of a plural form. Let me take an example: Being a monk of the Order of Cistercians, I have often been asked to expound 'Cistercian spirituality'. I have felt obliged to answer that I've no idea what such a thing might look like. The Cistercian project was from the outset a practical, evangelical enterprise. An early source, the *Exordium parvum*, written up in the 1120s, a quarter-century after monastic life had begun at Cîteaux, describes the founders' intention with these words: 'We have tirelessly borne the burden of the day and the heat so that [they who come after us] may sweat and toil even to the last gasp in the strait and narrow way which the Rule points out; till at last, having laid aside the burden of flesh, they happily repose in everlasting rest.' Novices were not introduced to 'Cistercian spirituality'. They were asked if they were willing to enter the paschal mystery of Christ Jesus in order to shed the Old Adam and put on the New.

The order has naturally, over the course of nearly a thousand years, accumulated a particular wisdom. There is naturally a characteristic way of life and prayer in our monasteries. We might even say that the Cistercian Order has come up with its own language for use in describing its heritage. The sum of all this is like a tapestry which, considered from a distance, resembles an icon of Christ. To excise individual threads from the woven whole, to separate them from structuring motifs such as conversion, the common life, liturgical prayers, silence, manual labour, and fasting, in order then to point to them as examples of 'Cistercian spirituality', is absurd. The projection has as little to do with the reality as a scent-of-the-woods incense stick in the loo of an elegant restaurant has to do with a genuine birch forest.

'Spirituality' comes from *spiritus*, which is Latin for both 'spirit' and 'breath': 'God is spirit' (John 4.24). 'Then the Lord God formed man from the dust of the ground, and breathed into his nostrils the breath of life; and the man became a living being' (Genesis 2.7). 'No one has ever seen God. It is God the only Son, who is close to the Father's heart, who has made him known' (John 1:18). Only on these terms is it meaningful to talk of 'spirituality'. Then the expression designates something specific: nature's encounter with the supernatural in Christ, the Father's wish to share his life and being with us in his Son, through the Spirit.

To live spiritually is to live in the Spirit attentively and obediently. The Spirit, Jesus told his disciples before he gave himself up to his Passion, will 'remind you of all that I have said to you' (John 14.26). A criterion of authentic 'spirituality' is this: It brings us closer to Christ and helps us to 'walk just as he walked' (1 John 2.6).

To be awakened to 'spirituality' is to awaken to responsibility and belonging. We find an account of how this comes about in a masterpiece of Nordic literature, Tito Colliander's cycle of memoirs in seven volumes, published between 1964 and 1973. The fourth volume, *Nära* [Coming Close], tells about the time Colliander spent in Estonia with his wife and children in the 30s. Born in 1904, Colliander had a sense of being in the middle of life. He was tired of what lay behind. He sought fresh experience, new words, 'a richer language, one more alive, a language able to embrace infinity and yet factual, dependable'. He found what he sought, though not in a brilliant concoction born of his own mind. No, it was the universe that started to speak to him. It spoke to him about the Word. He learnt to listen. In the utterances of things, he perceived with increasing clarity an echo of Scripture and of the Church's liturgy, in which the constant cry of *Kyrie eleison* vibrates with the jubilance of the angels' Gloria. The whole business was at once sublime and utterly concrete:

> The dung beetles rise on their hind legs and praise the Lord who gives them food: they can eat their fill of horse manure the blessed day long. 'Lord, my God, you are great and mighty. You are wrapt in light as in a robe, the clouds are your chariot, you travel on the wings of the wind'. Everything began to be pierced by truth and significance. Significance in every particular. Not merely in an interesting something, some historical or folkloric aspect. And not merely in my particularity, but in everyone's, everything's. A presence ever equal to itself, in all conditions and all circumstances the same. I began to believe in what I grasped of what surrounded me, of what I heard and read. With increasing strength I entertained the will to participate in everything that exists, that has been given to us all. A participant: that is what I wanted to become, not just a spectator in the wings.

Genuine spirituality awakens us like this. We touch the mystery indicated right at the end of scriptural revelation: 'The Spirit and the bride say, "Come." And let everyone who hears say, "Come"' (Revelation 22.17). The Spirit engages us. It gives us life in Jesus's name. It bids us give our life for our friends. We can't then be satisfied just to sit around. We intuit the connectedness of all there is. Each created being resonates with the eternal, life-giving Word of God – the beetle on its dungheap, I on mine.

Is it not time to free 'spirituality' from the introspective paradigm of self-help and to rediscover it as a category of theology, as a challenge to step out of our own shadow, towards the Light?

9

On Blessings

Blessings have become a subject of animated conversation in the Church. What is a blessing? According to the *Catechism*, it is 'a divine and life-giving action, the source of which is the Father; his blessing is both word and gift. When applied to man, the word "blessing" means adoration and surrender to his Creator in thanksgiving'. The opposite of a blessing (*benedictio*) is the curse (*maledictio*), issuing from humankind's attachment to sin, as at the time of Noah.

These terse definitions tell us much. A blessing worth its salt is a divine act. Originating from the Father, it is manifest as word (a term associated with the Son) and gift (a term associated with the Holy Spirit), Trinitarian in nature. By this act, grace is effectively transmitted to creatures. A human being, to receive God's blessing, must adore God and worship him in truth. He or she must 'surrender' to God, renouncing claims to self-sufficiency. This requires a resolve to break with sin, for sin leads to death, not life; it causes division, not integrity. Blessings are traditionally priestly. They presuppose an agent who is consecrated, wholly given to God, configured as an instrument of divine action.

How does blessing work? Let us consider a neutral example: the blessing of cheese (or butter) in the *Rituale Romanum* of Paul V, revised by Pius XI. It reads, 'Deign, almighty Lord God, to bless and sanctify this creature of cheese [or butter] which you have deigned to bring forth from animal fat, so that anyone from your faithful peoples who eats of it may, replete with your grace and heavenly benediction, be filled with good things. Through Christ, our Lord.' Uttering the words 'bless' and 'sanctify', the priest makes the sign of the cross upon the brie or butter, invoking the Trinity. The priest is not the originator of blessing. He invokes the blessing of God. He can do so because the delicious, nutritious substance before him represents a given perfection of created matter, produced by human ingenuity cooperating with providence. The cheese or butter realises God-given potential. Having blessed it, surrendering it in adoration to the Maker of all, the priest prays that it may bring benefit. The humble cheese or butter has by grace become a bearer of blessing.

There is, here, profound theology at work. God makes a creature (a cow) able to provide a particular good (milk). Human enterprise makes of this good something better (cheese or butter). This better thing is given back to God with a prayer that he, through the agency of an ordained minister, might accept it as his. The cheese-maker then receives the work of his or her own hands back as gift. To enter this logic of blessing is to enter an economy of grace. It is to learn to live graciously.

In the said *Rituale Romanum*, this structural paradigm is followed throughout. What constitutes a blessing is the priestly prayer that God might bless a thing or person in order that this thing or person may convey God's providential goodness and care. The blessing is enacted when the sign of the cross is set as a trinitarian seal upon the thing or person brought forward in oblation to be blessed. This same paradigm is followed in the beautiful blessings of water and salt for the asperges that occur in our current *Roman Missal*. Anyone can look them up there to verify what a blessing, in this strict sense, looks like.

If we turn to a more recent resource, the 1984 volume *De Benedictionibus*, a section of the *Rituale Romanum* promulgated by John Paul II, we encounter a different paradigm. A blessing for cheese or butter does not feature here. We might look instead at the blessing of work tools. After the initial rites ('In the name of the Father, and of the Son, and of the Holy Spirit'), a greeting, and an exhortation, the Word of God is read and, 'if opportune', expounded. There follow prayers of intercession. Then comes the Prayer of Blessing: 'God, from whom the fullness of blessing descends and to whom ascends the prayer of one who blesses, kindly protect your servants who with faithful devotion present to you their tools; grant that they, working zealously, may cooperate in the perfection of created things, sustain their lives and that of those entrusted to them, strive to further the progress of society, and ever praise the glory of your name. Through Christ our Lord.' There are marked contrasts to the formula cited above. There is no explicit prayer for God to bless. There is no indication that the sign of the cross is to be made. The rubrics lay down that this Prayer of Blessing can be read by a lay person as well as by a priest. The human subject is referred to as a 'blessing' subject. The tools brought forward are not, in fact, blessed. The 'blessing' consists in prayer for the people who will use the tools, that they might further the progress of society, etc.

We similarly find, in the *De Benedictionibus*, that the Prayer of Blessing for a new *cathedra* does not concern the object itself but 'those who will mount it'; the Prayer of Blessing over a church door concerns 'those who will enter through it'; even the Prayer of Blessing over animals is not about the beasts, but about us, 'that they might serve our good uses'. Such a Prayer of Blessing is clearly categorically distinct from the kind of blessing we found in the older prayer book, and still find in our Missal.

To my knowledge, this distinction has not been defined in a way apt to make it quite clear to the faithful, or, for that matter, to the clergy. Either category is referred to as a 'liturgical blessing' – a blessing, that is, of a type that a recent Declaration from the Dicastery for the Doctrine of the Faith, *Fiducia supplicans*, stressed may not be dispensed to 'couples in irregular situations'.

To such couples is held out, by contrast, the possibility of receiving a 'pastoral blessing' – that is, 'a blessing that, although not included in any liturgical rite, unites intercessory prayer with the invocation of God's help by those who humbly turn to him'. Such pastoral blessing is of its nature spontaneous and 'non-ritualised'. This being the case, the dicastery declared, on 18 December 2023, that 'no further responses should be expected about possible ways to regulate details or practicalities regarding blessings of this type'.

Those yet hoping for regulation have been joyfully fulfilled, however. On 4 January 2024, a "press release concerning the reception of *Fiducia supplicans*" was published by the dicastery. This text is most specific in showing the form a spontaneous, non-ritualised pastoral blessing should take. An example is 'imagined':

> Among a large number making a pilgrimage a couple of divorced people, now in a new union, say to the priest: 'Please give us a

blessing, we cannot find work, he is very ill, we do not have a home and life is becoming very difficult: may God help us!' In this case, the priest can recite a simple prayer like this: 'Lord, look at these children of yours, grant them health, work, peace and mutual help. Free them from everything that contradicts your Gospel and allow them to live according to your will. Amen'. Then it concludes with the sign of the cross on each of the two persons.

The text adds, 'We are talking about something that lasts about 10 or 15 seconds'. Given is an example not of blessing strictly speaking, but of kind attention and entreaty. The procedure is described as a gesture 'of pastoral closeness'. Insofar as an explicit act of blessing is envisaged, it is dispensed individually. No blessing is pronounced, in this instance, on the couple as such or on the individuals' union.

If this is what the dicastery intends when speaking, in *Fiducia supplicans*, of 'Blessings of Couples in Irregular Situations', have the debates surrounding this declaration in reality been much ado about nothing? Is it in fact 'blessings of couples' we are talking about? We shall see. Perhaps. Meanwhile, I believe three observations may be made with confidence.

First, there is widespread uncertainty about what a 'blessing' is; the term no longer has a universally accepted sense; exchanges have often been at cross-purposes. Second, clarity is unlikely to result from the accumulated attribution of qualifying adjectives or ad hoc commentary as long as key terms remain vague. Third, terminological vagueness generates confusion; confusion does not aid pastoral care or synodal progress, for it does not unite, but scatters, causing unrest. Human life is complex, not least where human affections, wounded by sin yet yearning for wholeness and health, are at stake. The Word became flesh not to bless our wounds but to heal them. He calls us 'out of darkness into his marvellous light' (1 Peter 2.9). He bore our sins to take them away. He does so still. By his still open wounds, we are healed (see 1 Peter 2.24).

The First Letter of Peter points out that we are called to 'inherit a blessing' (1 Peter 3.9). It tells us, 'In your hearts sanctify Christ as Lord. Always be ready to make your defence to anyone who demands from you an account of the hope that is in you' (1 Peter 3.15). Such accounting is the task of theology, known in earlier times as *regina scientiarum*, 'queen of the sciences', a discipline of compassion, yes, but also of intelligent precision, which cannot be reduced to an art of improvisation.

Regarding the theology of blessing, could not much be gained from owning afresh the radical sense of the term, letting it orient our lives, our worship, and our communities towards a finality of transformation, indeed of divinisation (see 2 Peter 1.4)? In our Missal's blessing of salt, the priest says, 'We humbly pray, almighty God, that you might deign in your faithful love to bless ✠ this creature of salt, which once you ordered the prophet Elisha to throw into water that the water's sterility might be healed. Grant, Lord, we pray, that wherever this mixture of salt and water shall be sprinkled, all the enemy's assaults having been cast out, the presence of your Holy Spirit may guard us always.'

Immersed in the tempestuous waters of this world, we are called to *be* salt (see Matthew 5.13).

10

Confirmation

The word 'confirmation' means, well, what it says: It denotes an action that strengthens and ratifies. Through this sacrament, God develops and makes definite a gift received in baptism. Candidates for confirmation declare their readiness to receive this gift and to live out its implications. They profess that they are full members of the Church's communion, prepared to assume responsibility for it – at least in principle.

In practice, alas, confirmation is often regarded at best as a formality, at worst as the conclusion of a young person's Catholic trajectory, pursued thus far under parental constraint. There is pertinence in the sour clerical joke which refers to confirmation as 'the last rite'. It matters all the more to focus on what this rite means, on what it accomplishes. Its significance is spelt out in the formula spoken by the bishop before he confers the sacrament. The liturgical translation is vague, so I venture to provide my own: 'Beloved, let us pray to God, the almighty Father, that he in his goodness would pour out his Holy Spirit on these adopted children of his, already reborn to eternal life in baptism. May the Spirit confirm them with the abundance of his gifts. May the Spirit, by his anointing, perfectly conform them to Christ, the Son of God.' It is affirmed that rebirth in the Spirit has already taken place. Those awaiting confirmation have been freed from sin's enslavement. They have by grace received a capacity for life eternal. What is about to take place is a strengthening through the Spirit's abundant gifts, named in their sevenfold perfection as 'the Spirit of Wisdom, Understanding, Counsel, Fortitude, Knowledge, Piety, and Fear of the Lord'. The Spirit's anointing is enacted by chrism, an ennobling substance whose purpose is configuration to Christ, God's Son. The outpouring of the Spirit has a Christocentric finality. The confirmed are to become Christlike and Christbearing. They are called to transformation, entrusted with a task.

How might this call, this mission be articulated? The scriptural text of reference in confirmation Masses is the account of Pentecost from Acts (2.1–13) with its tongues of flames and its speaking in tongues. Wonderful lessons can be drawn from it. Yet the chances are that the biblically estranged will find these apostolic phenomena too far out, beyond their reach, and possibly quite terrifying. It is helpful, then, to consider how the Apostles' proto-anointing was prepared and what were its effects, in order to enquire what Christomorphic life in the Spirit looks like over time.

We are struck by the newfound courage of the Twelve. After Pentecost, they proclaim the Resurrection in the face of brutal sanctions. They say, 'We must obey God rather than any human authority' (Acts 5.29), a statement made at considerable risk. This courage commands respect. It commands astonishment, too, when we reflect that the same group not long before sat huddled behind locked doors 'for fear of the Jews' (John 20.19), terrified of meeting the very same authorities they now openly challenge.

The Apostles' confirmation in the Spirit enabled such parrhesia. But let us not imagine that courage inevitably flows from a sacred rite, then or now. The Spirit is God, and God is no impersonal energy or automatic potency. He is a personal presence. To let a person into our lives, we must make a free decision. We may invade another person's attention and time. We may assail their nerves. But a relationship on these terms remains external. To gain access to another's heart, I need to be admitted freely, even as I am free to admit, or not, another to my heart. Not even God can force his way into my heart if I decide to close it. Our freedom at this level is absolute. That is part of the mystery of faith. No one can force us to love. No one can force us to be loved. And love is the foundation of our relationship with God.

Anointing with the Spirit presupposes the opening of hearts to love. A human heart cannot be prised open. It opens gradually, like a mussel revealing its pearl. The Apostles' hearts were carefully unsealed during the time between the Pasch and Pentecost. At first, after the trauma of Calvary, they sought to reestablish their lives as they had been before. They went fishing (John 21.3); that is, they returned to what they had been doing before their encounter with Jesus, which they thought had ended in a lamentable flop.

Yet there in the boat, in their reclaimed autonomy, the Lord sought them out. They saw with their own eyes that he who had been dead is alive. They ascertained that he is trustworthy, even in seemingly impossible matters. In the Gospel account, the relief of Peter and his friends is palpable.

Within their joy, however, floats a dark cloud – Peter's cloud.

Peter cannot forget that the last time he saw Jesus, he publicly said, not just once but three times, 'I've no idea who he is'. Nothing is harder to bear than the knowledge that I have betrayed someone I love, who loves me. How can Peter rejoice in the fact that Jesus is alive and receive his Spirit when he knows he has let him down cruelly?

Jesus knows what goes on in Peter's heart. He does not accuse him. Neither does he sweep the matter under an oriental rug. What he does do is this: He touches Peter's wound in such a way that it can heal. He asks three times, 'Do you love me?' (John 21.15–17). Thrice Peter is enabled to annul his denial. Peter comes across nervous, cowed, as if expecting a lash of the whip. What he meets instead is mercy. What is mercy? Readiness to look on others without illusions, conscious of their faults, and yet to love them.

Most of us struggle to believe we can be loved. We suppose that we, in order to be loveable, must first become something we are not. We make masks for ourselves. We try to appear the way we think we ought to be. Our true face we keep out of view. We think: If anyone saw that, they would run a mile and despise me.

Peter found, on behalf of us all, that it need not be like that. Jesus saw his sin and loved him nonetheless. Thus, he let Peter discover that he was still able to love. This was the source of the courage he showed thenceforth, from the day of Pentecost right into old age, when he freely laid down his life on Vatican Hill.

And this is the essence of what confirmation in the Spirit is about. To be anointed with the Spirit is to be seen and loved in truth for what I am and for what I have it in me to become, in order, then, to base my life on love. Jesus calls the Spirit 'the Spirit of truth' (John 16.13). To be confirmed is to pledge to found our existence on truth. God seals this purpose with his gift, enabling us to enter a covenant of faithfulness with him.

When life becomes serious – and it does – we need beacons to steer by, criteria to judge by. We need to tell the difference between black and white, truth and falsehood, good and evil. This challenge is urgent in our day. Europe is at war. We hear threats we thought the world would never hear again. No one knows what will happen. We are surrounded by influences wishing to steer and deceive us. We must choose sides, choose whom and what to obey. This holds not least for the young. The choices facing them are momentous. They need to know what they stand for.

In my experience, most of them realise this. They seek reliable coordinates. It is the Church's task, yours and mine, to bear witness that the grace of confirmation is one such coordinate, or rather, that it is the unfailing compass by which we can coordinate everything else.

I am tired of moans about the lapsing of the young. If the young leave the Church, it is not on account of bad will. It is because the claims of Christians seem irrelevant to the trials that await them. This calls for self-examination on the part of those of us who are adult Catholics. Do we live our Christ-conformed life in such a way that we merit the trust of the young? In this season, we should not just observe their confirmation. We should confirm our own anointing, reviving graces received.

We have declared once for all that we wish to do combat on the side of truth and mercy, under the banner of the cross, in the power of the Spirit. We received the Spirit's gift through the Church in the form of a cross traced on our forehead with sacred chrism. Let us be faithful to this sign, manifesting its promise. What our time needs is not more mushy rhetoric but confirmed witnesses.

Notes

Introduction

x   '**has traversed the depths of all the night**': Charles Péguy, *Le Porche du mystère de la deuxième vertu* (Gallimard, 1911).

Evangelisation in Forgetful Times

This chapter is developed from a paper given in Spanish as the Aquinas Lecture at the University of Navarra on 8 February 2024. The Spanish text has been published in the university's *Scripta Theologica*.

1   **Among the earliest outpourings of the human spirit to have been passed down to us is the *Epic of Gilgamesh***: Andrew George, trans., *The Epic of Gilgamesh* (Penguin, 1999).

3   '**modernity is characterised by an immense rage . . .**': François-Xavier Bellamy, *Demeure: Pour échapper à l'ère du mouvement perpétuel* (Grasset, 2018), 85. Bellamy's works have not been translated into English; it would be good if they were.

5   **Aristotle opposes what is *kath' holon* to what is *kath' hekaston***: Aristotle, *Analytica Posteriora*, A5, 74a4–12. Aristotle specifically addresses the quandary of *kath' holou* and *kath' hekaston*, a major theme in the *Analytica Posteriora*.

5   '**Marks of true Christian spirituality . . . *i.e.* hospitable**': Private correspondence between a nun of Stanbrook and the author. My reference to Sr. Gertrude Brown comes from this correspondence.

7   '**recognise, or better still, to *feel*, why Christianity is a possibility**': Navid Kermani, *Ungläubiges Staunen: Über das Christentum* (Beck, 2015), 10.

9   **Hebblethwaite calls Paul VI a 'modern pope' and 'modern man', and . . . 'modern' above all by implementing Vatican II**: Peter Hebblethwaite, *Paul VI: The First Modern Pope* (HarperCollins, 1993), 1. His triple celebration of modernity is right there on page 1.

NOTES

12 **An abbot, says Saint Benedict, is someone who brings forth from the store things 'both new and old':** Benedict of Nursia, 'The Election of an Abbot', chap. 64 in *The Rule*, in *St. Benedict Collection* (Word on Fire Classics, 2018). This passage on things new and old is in Saint Benedict's second disquisition on abbatial ministry.

13 **Pope Francis regularly affirmed . . . that we are living through 'not merely an epoch of change but a change of epoch':** Pope Francis, *Ad Theologiam Promovendam* 4 and 1, motu proprio, 1 November 2023, vatican.va. Pope Francis developed the theme of epochal change in several texts; but this is the one I here primarily have in mind.

15 **the ageing, ailing pope gave him a single counsel: 'Depositum custodi':** Peter Hebblethwaite, *Paul VI: The First Modern Pope* (HarperCollins, 1993), 260. This page includes the account of Montini's audience with Pius XII.

16 **the pope declared himself 'disturbed and saddened'. . . .** This and the following quotations are from Paul VI, *Sacrificium Laudis*, apostolic letter, 15 August 1966, vatican.va. Paul VI makes a plea to religious not precipitously to abandon the use of Latin in the liturgy in this apostolic letter. An English translation is published in *Documents on the Liturgy 1963–1979: Conciliar, Papal, and Curial Texts* by the International Commission on English in the Liturgy (Liturgical, 1982), 1080–81.

16 **'Customs and conventions change greatly as time passes. . . . But the heart of man changes not at all . . . ':** Sigrid Undset, *Fortællinger om Kong Artur og ridderne av det runde bord* (Aschehoug, 1915). This wistful thought about the human heart concludes Undset's book, published in English as *Tales of King Arthur*.

18 **Origen's . . . eagle eye saw the unfolding of events as a parable for the life of faith:** Origen of Alexandria, *Sermon 13*, in *Homélies sur la Genèse*, trans. Louis Doutreleau, Sources Chrétiennes 7, 2nd ed. (Cerf, 1976).

20 **Origen read that verse as pointing towards Christ the Morning Star:** Henri de Lubac, *Homélies sur l'Exode*, trans. P. Fortier, Sources Chrétiennes 16 (Cerf, 1947), 181. De Lubac's expostulation on the dawn is found as a footnote.

21 **Pope Benedict XV declared . . . the only way to confront with Christian**

integrity the end of civilisation was a determined focus on Christ's salvific action: Benedict XV, *Ad beatissimi apostolorum*, 1 November 1914, vatican.va.

21   **The guiding light . . . was the adage *Non nova, sed noviter*:** Benedict XV, *Ad beatissimi apostolorum*, 1 November 1914, vatican.va. The pontiff wrote, 'Ergo sanctam haberi volumus eam maiorum legem: Nihil innovetur, nisi quod traditum est; quae lex tametsi inviolate servanda est in rebus Fidei, tamen ad eius normam dirigenda sunt etiam, quae mutationem pati possunt; quamquam in his ea quoque regula plerumque valet: Non nova, sed noviter.'

Can Literature Saves Lives?

This chapter is based on a paper given at the Catholic Chaplaincy of the University of Cambridge on 25 April 2024, developing a Norwegian version published in my collection *Å finne sammen: politiske innspill* (St. Olav, 2023).

23   **Primo Levi reflects on the concentration camp's significance as an anthropological phenomenon:** Primo Levi, *Se questo è un uomo* (Einaudi, 1958). I have translated from this Italian edition, but the work is available in multiple published versions, of course.

29   **'Because I saw that my music was useless, *une musique inutile*':** Bruno Monsaingeon, dir. *Nadia Boulanger: Mademoiselle*. TF1, 1977. This film is available online.

30   **he called his diary secretly written up *A Journal of Happiness*:** Nicu Steinhardt, *Diario della felicitità*, trans. Gabriella Bertini Carageani (Redivide, 2017), 58–61.

32   **she conjures up the atmosphere in a vignette entitled 'In lieu of a foreword':** Anna Akhmatova, *Requiem*, in *The Complete Poems of Anna Akhmatova*, trans. Judith Hemschemeyer (Zephyr, 1992). See Akhmatova's prologue.

35   **the story of an important encounter: her reunion with Poppy:** Janet Frame, *An Angel at My Table: The Complete Autobiography*, 3 vols. (The Women's Press, 2001). The story of Poppy is told in chapters 9 and 21 of volume 1.

38   **'I'm a real bug for poetry . . .':** Zena Hitz, *Lost in Thought: The Hidden*

Pleasures of an Intellectual Life (Princeton University Press, 2020), 69. This work provided me with the quotation from Malcolm X, drawn from a letter to Philbert Little.

The Body at Prayer

This chapter is developed from a paper given at an ecumenical conference at Bjärka Säby on 6 September 2024.

41 **'I was led to Yoga by William of Saint-Thierry':** Jean Déchanet, *La Voie du silence* (Desclée de Brouwer, 1963). Déchanet's *La Voie du silence* went through several editions; I cite from the eleventh.

41–42 **Waddell amiably contrasts the perception of Bernard of Clairvaux with . . . Bernard Sylvestris:** Helen Waddell, *The Wandering Scholars* (Constable, 1927), chap. 3.

44 **He called Iyengar 'my best violin teacher':** Andrew Buncombe, 'BKS Iyengar: Teacher Who Spread Yoga Around the World and Numbered Menuhin, Huxley and Tendulkar Among His Followers', *The Independent*, 21 August 2014, https://www.the-independent.com/news/obituaries/bks-iyengar-teacher-who-spread-yoga-around-the-world-and-numbered-menuhin-huxley-and-tendulkar-among-his-followers-9684521.html. The account of Menuhin giving Iyengar a watch with the inscription 'To my best violin teacher' is cited in this obituary.

45 **'Reduced to our own body, our first instrument, we learn to play it':** Yehudi Menuhin, preface to *The Illustrated Light on Yoga*, by B. K. S. Iyengar (HarperCollins, 2004).

47 **Undset tells of the novel's hero Paul Selmer:** Sigrid Undset, *The Burning Bush*, trans. Arthur G. Chater (Cluny Classics, 2019). Paul Selmer's fasting is from book 2, chapter 2.

48 **'Give strength to my hands, Lord, to wipe away every stain . . .':** The priest's vesting prayers, previously printed in the *Missale Romanum*, can now be found, for instance, in the handy *Preces selectae* (Adams, 2001), 36f.

54 **The treatise . . . is redolent with the grace of the Word's Incarnation:** Dom

André Poisson, *La Prière du coeur par un chartreux* (La Correrie de la Grande Chartreuse, 2001). My English version can be accessed on the Carthusians' website: https://chartreux.org/moines/wp-content/uploads/2022/03/A-Carthusian-Prayer-of-the-Heart.pdf.

The Monastery as *SCHOLA DEI*

This chapter is developed from a paper given at a conference organised at Princeton by Princeton Initiative in Catholic Thought on 25–26 October 2024, under the title 'Beyond the Impasse: Theological Perspectives on DEI'.

57 Saint Benedict calls the monastery . . . *dominici schola servitii*: *RB 1980: The Rule of St. Benedict in Latin and English with Notes*, ed. Timothy Fry (Liturgical, 1981). I have indicated references using the standard edition, though I have here and there made minor adjustments, better to render the sense of the Latin.

58–59 like that of the Rusanovs in Solzhenitsyn's *Cancer Ward*: Solzhenitsyn's devastating but funny portrayal of the Rusanovs occurs towards the end of the fourteenth chapter, entitled 'Justice', of part 1 of *Cancer Ward*. Catholics may wish to replace 'People' with 'Church' in this passage, then reread it in view of an examination of conscience.

64–65 'Equity refers to fair treatment for all people . . .': 'What Is Diversity, Equity, and Inclusion?' McKinsey & Company, 17 August 2022, https://www.mckinsey.com/featured-insights/mckinsey-explainers/what-is-diversity-equity-and-inclusion.

69 There is something Terentian about monasticism. The dictum 'Nothing human is foreign to me' is reflected . . .: Terence, *Heauton Timorumenos* 1.1.77. Here we find Terence's oft-cited phrase 'Humani nil a me alienum puto'.

69 Murmuring is a form of passive aggression . . .: Anyone wanting a fuller disquisition on the phenomenon of murmuring can find it in a dedicated chapter of Erik Varden, *Entering the Twofold Mystery: On Christian Conversion* (Bloomsbury, 2022).

Repairing the Wound

This chapter is developed from a paper given at the Catholic cathedral in Oslo on 3 November 2021.

75   'Je suis une morte vivante pour la vie': *Sauvé Report* (Independent Commission on Sexual Abuse in the Church), published 5 October 2021, https://www.ciase.fr.

76   **Ignatius calls the Eucharist . . . 'the medicine of immortality'**: Ignatius develops the theme of φάρμακον ἀθανασίας in chapter 20 of *Letter to the Ephesians*.

77   **'Forgive me, brethren. . . . Let me receive the pure light . . .'**: His hope to receive 'pure light' is expressed in chapter 6 of his *Letter to the Romans*.

78   **'If you would like to visit a place where the symptoms of the sickness of our time . . .'**: John Waters, 'Ireland: An Obituary', *First Things*, 28 May 2018, https://firstthings.com/ireland-an-obituary/.

82–83   **'Christ remains in agony until the end of time . . .'**: Blaise Pascal, *Pensées*, vol. 2, ed. León Brunschvicg (Hachette, 1904), no. 553, p. 435: 'Jésus sera en agonie jusqu'à la fin du monde. Il ne faut pas dormir pendant ce temps-là'.

'Be Holy!': The Scandal of Sanctity

This chapter is developed from a paper given as the Saint William of York Lecture at the University of York on 11 December 2024. I could not resist remarking, in that setting, that a church in York was dedicated to Saint Olav in 1055, just twenty-five years after he was killed, proof of the rapid spread of his cult.

92   **Sacks sets out from Moses's passion for justice**: Jonathan Sacks, 'Of What Was Moses Afraid', Covenant & Conversation series, https://rabbisacks.org/covenant-conversation/shemot/of-what-was-moses-afraid/. Moses's 'Here I am' at the burning bush is the same answer candidates for ordination give when called, before the Church, to formalise their free, definitive self-oblation.

95–96   **'I rushed to her bedside. She was still breathing . . .'**: Paul Glynn, *A Song for Nagasaki: The Story of Takashi Nagai* (Ignatius, 2009). Quotations used from Nagai are found on pages 34, 39, 137, 160, 173, 185ff., 225.

96 'Our wretchedness is that of a dispossessed king': Blaise Pascal, *Pensées*, vol. 2, ed. León Brunschvicg (Hachette, 1904), no. 398, p. 303: 'Toutes ces misères-là même prouvent sa grandeur. Ce sont misères de grand seigneur, misères d'un roi déposédé.

103 The *Mémorial* begins with a monosyllabic exclamation: *Feu!*: Blaise Pascal, *Pensées*, vol. 1, ed. León Brunschvicg (Hachette, 1904), p. 3. The full *Mémorial* appears on pp. 3–7.

Synodality and Holiness

This chapter is developed from a paper given to the General Chapter of the Congregation of Solesmes on 27 April 2023.

105 Observers have argued that the ... synod's vision is like the overflowing of the council's cup: Michael Sean Winters, 'Synodal Working Document Is Deeply Rooted in Vatican II', *The National Catholic Reporter*, 26 June 2023, https://www.ncronline.org/opinion/ncr-voices/synodal-working-document-deeply-rooted-vatican-ii.

105 Cardinal Grech ... conceding that the word 'synodality' is absent from the council's documents but submitting it arises therefrom ...: Cindy Wooden, 'Dream of 'Synodality' Is a Fruit of Vatican II, Cardinal Writes', *The Catholic Review*, 11 October 2022, https://catholicreview.org/dream-of-synodality-is-a-fruit-of-vatican-ii-cardinal-writes/.

105 'dynamic' rather than 'static': Bernadette Mary Reis, 'Sr Nathalie to Suva Assembly: "You Are on Forefront of Synodality"', *Vatican News*, 7 February 2023, https://www.vaticannews.va/en/church/news/2023-02/nathalie-becquart-continental-assembly-suva-synodality-oceania.html.

106 'All the faithful of Christ are invited to strive for the holiness and perfection of their own proper state ...': Second Vatican Council, *Lumen gentium* 42, 21 November 1964, vatican.va.

107 Saint Benedict saw the type of such circularity, the *gyrovague*, as the ultimate loser: *RB 1980: The Rule of St. Benedict in Latin and English with Notes*, ed. Timothy Fry (Liturgical Press, 1981). Saint Benedict's teaching on gyrovagues, already considered in chapter 4, is in chapter 1 of the *Rule*.

114 **'Since Jesus, the Son of God, manifested His charity . . .'**: Second Vatican Council, *Lumen gentium* 42, 21 November 1964, vatican.va.

114 **the path of the commandments**: See the end of the prologue to Saint Benedict's *Rule*.

114–115 **'man will perceive the history of this world . . . as an immense symphony'**: Elisabeth Paule Labat, *Essai sur le mystère de la musique* (Fleurus, 1963). Elisabeth-Paule Labat (1897–1975) was a nun of Saint Michel de Kergonan. Her *Essai sur le mystère de la musique*, published in 1963, is remarkable. My English translation was published by Liturgical Press in 2014 under the title *The Song That I Am: On the Mystery of Music*. The passage cited is from the last part of the chapter on 'Music and Liturgy'.

Setting 'Spirituality' Free

This chapter is developed from a text originally written in Norwegian as an introduction to the volume *Kristen spiritualitet og teologi*, ed. by Ståle Johannes Kristiansen and Kim Larsen (Novus, 2024).

117 **'We have tirelessly borne the burden of the day and the heat . . .'**: *Exordium parvum*. The *Exordium parvum* is available in Latin and English on the website of the Order of Cistercians of the Strict Observance: https://ocso.org/resources/foundational-text/exordium-parvum/.

119 **'a richer language, one more alive, a language able to embrace infinity . . .'**: Tito Colliander, 'Ljuslågorna', in *Nära* (Schildts, 1971), 172, 177. For years it has been a puzzle to me that the writings of Tito Colliander, short of *The Way of the Ascetics*, have never been translated into English. His suite of memoirs is wonderful.

On Blessings

This chapter is developed from an essay written in an attempt to make sense of the Dicastery for the Doctrine of the Faith's declaration *Fiducia supplicans* of 18 December 2023. I published the piece on my website on 5 January 2024: https://coramfratribus.com/life-illumined/on-blessings-again/.

121 '**a divine and life-giving action, the source of which is the Father . . .**': *Catechism of the Catholic Church* 1078.

121 **issuing from humankind's attachment to sin, as at the time of Noah**: *Catechism of the Catholic Church* 1080.

122 '**Deign, almighty Lord God, to bless and sanctify . . .**': Paul V, *Rituale Romanum*, 1614.

125–126 **Human life is complex, not least where human affections, wounded by sin by sin yet yearning for wholeness and health, are at stake:** For a fuller treatment on this theme, see Erik Varden, *Chastity: Reconciliation of the Senses* (Bloomsbury, 2023).

Confirmation

This chapter is developed from an essay published in *The Tablet* on 23 March 2024 as part of a series on the sacraments. It is reproduced by gracious permission of the editor.